Booksellers on *Tell Me How It Ends*

"With gifted prose and a compassionate but penetrating gaze, Luiselli personalizes the ongoing plight of Latin American child migrants in the United States. Her own immersion as a translator informs a trenchant first-hand account of the labyrinthine legal processes and inevitable bureaucratic indifference faced by undocumented youth. Humane yet often horrifying, *Tell Me How It Ends* offers a compelling, intimate look at a continuing crisis—and its ongoing cost in an age of increasing urgency."
—Jeremy Garber, Powell's Books

"In the hours Valeria Luiselli spends at the immigration courts in NYC, her duty is to listen to children tell her stories about their scars and how they got them. Like a morbid game show, the children's answers determine their fate. The grand prize? Permanent citizenship, if all goes well. The alternative? Deportation. Bonus: due to the volume of cases, the standard intake form forgives only those who have the most gruesome traumas, wounds that they can show—and, of course, the language to speak about them. Part treatise, part memoir, part call to action, *Tell Me How It Ends* inspires not through a stiff stance of authority, but with the curiosity and humility Luiselli has long since established. It may not cure your panic, but it sure as hell won't feed it."
—Annalia Luna, Brazos Bookstore

"'Tell me how it ends,' the young daughter says to the mother. Valeria Luiselli uses this query, said of the heartbreaking, infuriating situation involving 'undocumented' Central American children and the legal system they encounter here that she movingly chronicles in this powerful essay. She helps call to question where we as people, as a people, are with innocent children, who or what is 'alien,' even the business of who is American, given that she casts this as a connective scenario, with what happens in Tegucigalpa being related to what happens in Hempstead, New York. In this we are all Americans, finally. Imagine being put into court systems without the language to speak, much less the adult language of law. And while this essay is brilliant for exactly what it depicts, it helps open larger questions, which we're ever more on the precipice of now, of where all of *this* will go, how all of *this* might end. Is this a story, or is this beyond a story? Valeria Luiselli is one of those brave and eloquent enough to help us see."
—Rick Simonson, Elliott Bay Book Company

"Valeria Luiselli's *Tell Me How It Ends* helped me see the crisis undocumented immigrants, especially children coming from Mexico and Central America, are facing in our country in much the same way Michelle Alexander's *The New Jim Crow* helped me see how slavery's legacy is being perpetuated in the mass incarceration of black Americans. As someone who has read every one of Luiselli's books, I expected her writing here to be erudite and elegant, and it is, of course it is, but what I did not expect was for her writing to be this immediate and this personal. I did not expect to be hit this hard emotionally, to feel every fear and every longing in the deepest part of who I am. I can't remember the last time I read something and had this kind of physical reaction. I felt this book in the tug behind my eyes, in these hands shaking, in this heart beating too quickly. This is a work I will share with everyone I know. This is something every American needs to face, and to feel."　　　　　　　　　　　　—Kenny Coble, King's Books

"In an essay as bracing as it is searing, the incomparable Valeria Luiselli explores the 2014 immigration crisis. Luiselli writes with a clarity that underscores the nightmarish conditions and nonsensical bureaucracy undocumented children face on their passage to America and toward u.s. citizenship. *Tell Me How It Ends* evokes empathy as it educates. It is a vital contribution to the body of post-Trump work being published in early 2017."

—Katharine Solheim, Unabridged Bookstore

"Valeria Luiselli's extended essay on her volunteer work translating for child immigrants confronts with compassion and honesty the problem of the North American refugee crisis. It's a rare thing: a book everyone should read."

—Stephen Sparks, Point Reyes Books

"Books like *Tell Me How It Ends* are like dew on a spiderweb, revealing the often forgotten and sometimes ignored threads of humanity that connect us all. Luiselli introduces us to one of the forgotten figures and tragic heroes of contemporary America: the child who risked everything to come here. Through stories about specific children, personal reflection, and consideration of our immigration system, Luiselli sheds light on what most of us would choose to ignore and gives new meaning to the question, Why are we here?"

—Josh Cook, Porter Square Books

"Compelling and urgent, *Tell Me How It Ends* gives a face and a name to the hundreds of thousands who have committed the innocent crime of geography: being born in a certain time and place. The bureaucratic labyrinth of immigration, the dangers of searching for a better life, all of this and more is contained in this brief and profound work. *Tell Me How It Ends* is not just relevant, it's essential."　　　　　　　　　　　　—Mark Haber, Brazos Bookstore

"Valeria Luiselli's *Tell Me How It Ends* is an important reminder that words matter. The questions we ask of others are built upon a foundation of assumptions about the past and expectations for the future. Appealing to the language of the United States' fraught immigration policy, Luiselli exposes the cracks in this foundation. Herself an immigrant, she highlights the human cost of its brokenness, as well as the hope that it (rather than walls) might be rebuilt."

—Brad Johnson, Diesel Bookstore

TELL ME
HOW IT
ENDS

TELL ME
HOW IT
ENDS

AN ESSAY IN
FORTY
QUESTIONS

VALERIA
LUISELLI

COFFEE HOUSE PRESS
Minneapolis
2017

Coffee House Press books are available to the trade through our primary distributor, Consortium Book Sales & Distribution, cbsd.com or (800) 283-3572. For personal orders, catalogs, or other information, write to info@coffeehousepress.org.

Coffee House Press is a nonprofit literary publishing house. Support from private foundations, corporate giving programs, government programs, and generous individuals helps make the publication of our books possible. We gratefully acknowledge their support in detail in the back of this book.

LIBRARY OF CONGRESS CATALOGING-IN-PUBLICATION DATA

Names: Luiselli, Valeria, 1983– author.
Title: Tell me how it ends : an essay in 40 questions / Valeria Luiselli.
Description: Minneapolis : Coffee House Press, 2017. | Includes bibliographical references and index.
Identifiers: LCCN 2017000414 | ISBN 9781566894951 (softcover)
Subjects: LCSH: Immigrant children—United States—Social conditions. | Illegal alien children—United States—Social conditions. | Immigrant children—Legal status, laws, etc.—United States. | Illegal alien children—Legal status, laws, etc.—United States. | United States—Emigration and immigration—Government policy. | BISAC: LITERARY COLLECTIONS / Essays. | SOCIAL SCIENCE / Emigration & Immigration. | POLITICAL SCIENCE / Civics & Citizenship. | POLITICAL SCIENCE / Globalization.
Classification: LCC JV6600 .L85 2017 | DDC 305.23086/9120973—dc23
LC record available at https://lccn.loc.gov/2017000414

Acknowledgments

A shorter version of this essay was originally written in English and appeared in *Freeman's* in 2016. The author then rewrote the essay in Spanish and, while doing so, expanded upon it. That version was published as *Los niños perdidos (Un ensayo en cuarenta preguntas)* by Sexto Piso in 2016. The new sections of the essay were translated into English by Lizzie Davis, in consultation with the author.

PRINTED IN THE UNITED STATES OF AMERICA

25 24 23 22 21 20 19 18   11 12 13 14 15 16 17 18

TELL ME
HOW IT
ENDS

INTRODUCTION

In **Tell Me How It Ends** *there are no answers, only more questions.* In this urgent, haunting, exquisitely written little book, the questions asked by Valeria Luiselli are her own, her children's, and those she finds on the questionnaire drawn up by immigration attorneys for the tens of thousands of Central American children who arrive in the United States each year after being smuggled across Mexico to the U.S. border. These children are the most vulnerable members of an ongoing exodus of Central Americans fleeing poverty and violence in their shattered nations in the expectation of finding a better life in the United States. Many of the children are raped, robbed, or even killed along the way.

As a Mexican woman living in the United States, facing her own travails with the immigration service for a green card that would grant her U.S. residency and permission to work, Luiselli became transfixed by the surge of child refugees during the summer of 2014. She began working as an interpreter with an immigration court in New York City, where she was given the task of assisting the children with the intake questionnaire, asking its questions of them in Spanish and then translating their answers. Depending on those answers, they might or might not be granted legal sanctuary of some sort—and thus a future—in the United States. Luiselli soon realized it was impossible to fit the children's lives neatly into the boxes provided, observing, "The children's stories are always shuffled, stuttered, always shattered beyond the repair of a narrative order. The problem with trying to tell their story is that it has no beginning, no middle, and no end."

The result of Luiselli's experience is this book, in which the questions posed to the refugee children become catalysts for her own questions about the nature of family, childhood, and community, and above all, about national identity and belonging. She offers a fascinating rumination on the complex nature of the attraction of the United States for the refugee children and their families—and even for herself—despite its unwelcoming nature, casual racism, and official disinterest in their very existence. "Before coming to the United States, I knew what others know: that the cruelty of its borders was only a thin crust, and that on the other side a possible life was waiting," she concludes. "I understood, some time after, that once you stay here long enough, you begin to remember the place where you originally came from the way a backyard might look from a high window in the deep of winter: a skeleton of the world, a tract of abandonment, objects dead and obsolete. And once you're here, you're ready to give everything, or almost everything, to stay and play a part in the great theater of belonging."

Luiselli's book appears during an especially raw juncture in the relationship between her birthplace, Mexico, and her adoptive home, the United States. During the 2016 U.S. presidential election campaign, the nature of the relationship between the two countries became an essential plank in the candidacy of Republican billionaire Donald Trump, who notoriously referred to Mexicans as unwelcome intruders, as "criminals, drug dealers, and rapists" and called for a wall to be built along the border, one that, in an apparent effort to be as humiliating as possible, he insisted "Mexico will pay for."

In this hallucinatory global political climate, in which bigoted notions about national identity, sect, and race have reared their heads to a degree not seen in many decades, Trump's statements gained him a sizeable American following. It is distressingly clear that the fears and hatreds he has unleashed—especially since he, and not Hillary Clinton, won the election to become president—will not be easily put to rest. What does this mean for the refugee children and their families who flee shattered communities to the United States, hoping to make themselves whole again? Luiselli does not know, but she feels certain that whatever their reception in the United States, the children will keep coming as long as there is a need to escape from realities too frightening to bear. "Children run and flee. They have an instinct for survival, perhaps, that allows them to endure almost anything just to make it to the other side of horror, whatever may be waiting there for them." And what awaits them is a bewildering and often daunting reality, with little in the way of guidance to help them adapt. After six months adjusting to life in a tough neighborhood of New York, one Honduran youngster tells Luiselli what he has learned thus far: his new home "is a shithole full of pandilleros, just like Tegucigalpa."

In the course of her work, Luiselli's young daughter has heard about some of the children's stories, and she repeatedly asks, as children do, "Tell me how it ends, Mamma." Luiselli has no answers for her. There are, as yet, no happy endings, but toward the end of the book she offers a small hint of promise. It comes in the form of a decision by ten young Americans, just a few years older than the children of the intake questionnaires, to form a group that will help teenage refugees who have made it to the United States and managed to stay.

This is a profoundly moving book, one that, with its modest hundred pages and simple, teasing title, presents itself as a mere story guided by forty questions. But

4

appearances are, after all, beguiling, and this is a most powerful story, beautifully told by Valeria Luiselli. I feel sure that whoever reads it will not regret it, nor easily forget it.

Jon Lee Anderson
Dorset, England
January 14, 2017

I

BORDER

"Why did you come to the United States?" That's the first question on the intake questionnaire for unaccompanied child migrants. The questionnaire is used in the federal immigration court in New York City where I started working as a volunteer interpreter in 2015. My task there is a simple one: I interview children, following the intake questionnaire, and then translate their stories from Spanish to English.

But nothing is ever that simple. I hear words, spoken in the mouths of children, threaded in complex narratives. They are delivered with hesitance, sometimes distrust, always with fear. I have to transform them into written words, succinct sentences, and barren terms. The children's stories are always shuffled, stuttered, always shattered beyond the repair of a narrative order. The problem with trying to tell their story is that it has no beginning, no middle, and no end.

When the intake interview with a child is over, I meet with lawyers to deliver and explain my transcription and occasional notes. The lawyers then analyze the child's responses, trying to come up with options for a viable defense against a child's deportation and the "potential relief" he or she is likely to get. The next step is to find legal representation. Once an attorney has agreed to take on a case, the real legal battle begins. If that battle is won, the child will obtain some form of immigration relief. If it is lost, they will receive a deportation order from a judge.

I watch our own children sleep in the back seat of the car as we cross the George Washington Bridge into New Jersey. I glance back now and then from the copilot's seat at my ten-year-old stepson, visiting us from Mexico, and my five-year-old daughter. Behind the wheel, my husband concentrates on the road ahead.

It is the summer of 2014. We are waiting for our green cards to be either granted or denied and, in the meantime, we decide to go on a family road trip. We will drive from Harlem, New York, to a town in Cochise County, Arizona, near the U.S.-Mexico border.

According to the slightly offensive parlance of U.S. immigration law, for the three years or so that we had lived in New York we had been "nonresident aliens." That's the term used to describe anyone from outside the United States—"alien"—whether or not they are residents. There are "nonresident aliens," "resident aliens," and even "removable aliens"—that I know of. We wanted to become "resident aliens," even though we knew what applying for green cards implied: the lawyers, the expenses, the many vaccinations and medical exams, the months of sustained uncertainty, the rather humiliating intermediate steps, such as having to wait for an "advance parole" document in order to be able to leave the country and be paroled back in, like a criminal, as well as the legal prohibition against traveling abroad, without losing immigration status, before being granted advance parole. Despite all that, we decided to apply.

When we finally sent out our applications, a few weeks before leaving for our road trip, we started feeling strange, somewhat out of place, a little circumspect—as if throwing that envelope in the blue mailbox on our street corner had changed something in us. We joked, somewhat frivolously, about the possible definitions of our new, now pending, migratory status. Were we "pending aliens," or "writers seeking status," or "alien writers," or maybe "pending Mexicans"? I suppose, deeper down, we were simply asking ourselves, perhaps for the first time, that same question I now ask children at the beginning of each intake interview: "Why did you come to the United States?"

We didn't have a clear answer. No one ever does. But the deed was done, we had filed our applications, and while we waited for an answer we were not allowed to leave the country. So, when summer arrived, we bought maps, rented a car, packed a few basics, made playlists, and left New York.

The green card application is nothing like the intake questionnaire for undocumented minors. When you apply for a green card you have to answer things like "Do you intend to practice polygamy?" and "Are you a member of the Communist Party?" and "Have you ever knowingly committed a crime of moral turpitude?" And although nothing can or should be taken lightly when you are in the fragile situation of asking for permission to live in a country that is not your own, there is something almost innocent in the green card application's preoccupations with and visions of the future and its possible threats: polyamorous debauchery, communism, weak morals! The green card questionnaire has a retro kind of candor, like the grainy Cold War films we watched on VHS. The intake questionnaire for undocumented children, on the other hand, reveals a colder, more cynical and brutal reality. It reads as if it were written in high definition, and as you make your way down its forty questions it's impossible not to feel that the world has become a much more fucked-up place than anyone could have ever imagined.

The process by which a child is asked questions during the intake interview is called screening, a term that is as cynical as it is appropriate: the child a reel of footage, the translator-interpreter an obsolete apparatus used to channel that footage, the legal system a screen, itself too worn out, too filthy and tattered to allow any clarity, any attention to detail. Stories often become generalized, distorted, appear out of focus.

Before the formal screening begins, the person conducting it has to fill in basic biographical information: the child's name, age, and country of birth, the name of a sponsor in the United States, the people with whom he or she is living at the time, and a contact number and address. All these details have to be written down at the very top of the questionnaire.

A few spaces down, right before the first formal interview question, a line floats across the page like an uncomfortable silence:

Where is the child's mother?_____father?_____

The interviewer has to write down whatever information the child can or will give to fill in those blanks—those two empty spaces that look a bit like badly stitched wounds. Too often, the spaces remain blank: all the children come without their fathers and mothers. And many of them do not even know where their parents are.

We are driving across Oklahoma in early July when we first hear about the wave of children arriving, alone and undocumented, at the border. On our long west-bound drives we begin to follow the story on the radio. It's a sad story that hits so close to home and yet seems completely unimaginable, almost unreal: tens of thousands of children from Mexico and Central America have been detained at the border. Nothing is clear in the initial coverage of the situation—which soon becomes known, more widely, as an immigration crisis, though others will advocate for the more accurate term "refugee crisis."

Questions, speculations, and opinions flash-flood the news during the days that follow. Who are these children? What will happen to them? Where are the parents? Where will they go next? And why, why did they come to the United States?

"Why did you come to the United States?" I ask children in immigration court.

Their answers vary, but they often point to a single pull factor: reunification with a parent or another close relative who migrated to the u.s. years earlier. Other times, the answers point to push factors—the unthinkable circumstances the children are fleeing: extreme violence, persecution and coercion by gangs, mental and physical abuse, forced labor, neglect, abandonment. It is not even the American Dream that they pursue, but rather the more modest aspiration to wake up from the nightmare into which they were born.

Then comes question number two in the intake questionnaire: "When did you enter the United States?" Most children don't know the exact date. They smile and say "last year" or "a few months ago" or simply "I don't know." They've fled their towns and cities; they've walked and swum and hidden and run and mounted freight trains and trucks. They've turned themselves in to Border Patrol officers. They've come all this way looking for—for what, exactly? The questionnaire doesn't make these other inquiries. But it does ask for precise details: "When did you enter the United States?"

As we drive deeper into the country, following the enormous map I take from the glove box and study from time to time, the summer heat becomes drier, the light thinner and whiter, the roads more solitary. We start hunting down any available information about the undocumented children and the situation at the border. We collect local newspapers, which pile on the floor of our car, in front of my copilot seat. We do constant, quick online searches and tune in to the radio every time we can catch a signal.

More questions, speculations, and opinions flood media coverage of the crisis: some sources elaborate lucid and complex conjectures on the origin and possible causes of the sudden surge of arrivals of unaccompanied minors, others denounce the inhumane conditions and systematic maltreatment the children must endure in detention facilities near the border, and a few others endorse the spontaneous civilian protests against them.

A caption in a web publication explains an unsettling photograph of men and women waving flags, banners, and rifles in the air: "Protesters, some exercising their open-carry rights, assemble outside of the Wolverine Center in Vassar [Michigan] that would house illegal juveniles to show their dismay for the situation." In another photograph that we find on the web, an elderly couple holds signs saying "Illegal Is a Crime" and "Return to Senders." They are sitting on beach chairs, wearing sunglasses. A caption explains, "Thelma and Don Christie (C) of Tucson demonstrate against the arrival of undocumented immigrants in Oracle, Arizona. July 15, 2014." I zoom in on their faces and wonder. What passed through the minds of Thelma and Don Christie when they prepared their protest signs? Did they pencil in "protest against illegal immigrants" on their calendars, right next to "mass" and just before "bingo"? What were they thinking when they put their beach chairs inside their trunk? And what did they talk about as they drove the forty miles or so north, toward the protest in Oracle?

In varying degrees, some papers and webpages announce the arrival of undocumented children like a biblical plague. Beware the locusts! They will cover the face of the ground so that it cannot be seen—these menacing, coffee-colored boys and girls, with their obsidian hair and slant eyes. They will fall from the skies, on our cars, on our green lawns, on our heads, on our schools, on our Sundays. They will make a racket, they will bring their chaos, their sickness, their dirt, their brownness. They will cloud the pretty views, they will fill the future with bad omens, they will fill our tongues with barbarisms. And if they are allowed to stay here they will—eventually—reproduce!

We wonder if the reactions would be different were all these children of a lighter color: of better, purer breeds and nationalities. Would they be treated more like people? More like children? We read the papers, listen to the radio, see photographs, and wonder.

In a diner near Roswell, New Mexico, we overhear a conversation between a waitress and a customer. As she refills his coffee, she tells him that hundreds of migrant kids will be put on private planes—rumored to have been funded by a patriotic millionaire—and deported that same day back to Honduras, or Mexico, or somewhere. The planes full of "alien" children will leave from an airport not far from the famous UFO museum, the one our children have been set on visiting. The term "alien," which only a few weeks ago made us laugh and speculate, which we had been passing around the car as an inside family joke, is suddenly shown to us under a bleaker light. It's strange how concepts can erode so easily, how words we once used lightly can alchemize abruptly into something toxic.

The next day, driving out of Roswell, we look for news on what happened with those deportees. We find no details of the exact circumstances under which they were deported, or how many there were, and if it's true that a local millionaire financed their removal. We do, however, come across these lines in a Reuters report that read like the beginning of a cruel, absurdist story by Mikhail Bulgakov or Daniil Kharms: "Looking happy, the deported children exited the airport on an over-cast and sweltering afternoon. One by one, they filed into a bus, playing with balloons they had been given." We dwell for a while on the adjective "happy" and the strangely meticulous description of the local weather in San Pedro Sula, Honduras: "an overcast and sweltering afternoon." But what we really cannot stop reproducing, somewhere in the dark back of our minds, is the uncanny image of the children holding those balloons.

In our long daily drives, to fill in the empty hours, we sometimes tell our children stories about the old

American Southwest, back when it used to be part of Mexico. I tell them about Saint Patrick's Battalion, the group of Irish Catholic soldiers who joined the u.s. Army as cannon fodder during the Mexican-American War, but later changed sides to fight along with the Mexicans. I tell them about the Treaty of Guadalupe Hidalgo, signed after that war, in which Mexico lost half its territory to the United States. Their father tells them about President Andrew Jackson's Indian Removal Act, approved by Congress in 1830, and explains how it brutally exiled Native Americans to reservations. He tells them about Geronimo, Cochise, Mangas Coloradas, and the other Chiricahua Apaches: the last inhabitants of a continent to surrender to the white-eyes, after years of battle against both the u.s. Bluecoats and the Mexican Army. Those last Chiricahua resisted for many more years after the Indian Removal Act was passed. They finally surrendered in 1886 and were "removed" to the San Carlos Reservation—in southern Arizona, toward which we are now driving. It's curious, or perhaps just sinister, that the word "removal" is still used to refer to the deportation of "illegal" immigrants—those bronzed barbarians who threaten the white peace and superior values of the "Land of the Free."

When we run out of stories to tell our children, we fall silent and look out at the unbroken line of the highway, perhaps trying to put together the many pieces of the story—the unimaginable story—unfolding just outside the small and protected world of our rented car. Though all of it resists a rational explanation, we talk it over and consider its many angles. We try to answer our own children's questions about the situation as best we can. But we don't do very well. How do you explain any of this to your own children?

The third and fourth questions on the intake questionnaire are ones that our children, too, ask many times, though in their own words: "With whom did you travel to this country?" and "Did you travel with anyone you knew?" All children travel with a paid coyote. Some of them travel also with siblings, cousins, and friends.

Sometimes, when our children fall asleep again, I look back at them, or hear them breathe, and wonder if they would survive in the hands of coyotes and what would happen to them if they were deposited at the U.S. border, left either on their own or in the custody of Border Patrol officers. Were they to find themselves alone, crossing borders and countries, would my own children survive?

The fifth and sixth questions are: "What countries did you pass through?" and "How did you travel here?" To the first one, almost everyone immediately answers "Mexico," and some also list Guatemala, El Salvador, and Honduras. To the question about how they traveled here, with a blend of pride and horror, most say, "I came on La Bestia," which literally means "the beast," and refers to the freight trains that cross Mexico, on top of which as many as half a million Central American migrants ride annually. There are no passenger services along the routes, so migrants have to ride atop the railcars or in the recesses between them.

Thousands have died or been gravely injured aboard La Bestia, either because of the frequent derailments of the old freight trains or because people fall off during the night. The most minor oversight can be fatal. Some compare La Bestia to a demon, others to a kind of vacuum that sucks distracted riders down into its metal entrails. And when the train itself is not the threat, it's the smugglers, thieves, policemen, or soldiers who frequently threaten, blackmail, or attack the people on board. There is a saying about La Bestia: Go in alive, come out a mummy.

But, despite the dangers, people continue to take the risk. Children certainly take the risk. Children do what their stomachs tell them to do. They don't think twice when they have to chase a moving train. They run along with it, reach for any metal bar at hand, and fling themselves toward whichever half-stable surface they may land on. Children chase after life, even if that chase might end up killing them. Children run and flee. They have an instinct for survival, perhaps, that allows them

19

to endure almost anything just to make it to the other side of horror, whatever may be waiting there for them.

La Bestia's routes start either in the town of Tapachula, in the state of Chiapas, or in Tenosique, in the state of Tabasco—both towns near the Mexico-Guatemala border. They slowly make their way up to the U.S.-Mexico border, following either the eastern Gulf route to Reynosa, the border town near the southeastern-most tip of Texas, or the western routes that lead either to Ciudad Juárez, in Chihuahua, or to Nogales, in Sonora, which share borders with Texas, Arizona, and New Mexico.

The journey atop La Bestia's freight trains ends at the U.S.-Mexico border. And there begins another journey: one that is not as dangerous, objectively speaking, but is equally terrifying in the children's eyes. Once off La Bestia, and having reached the border, the coyotes' job is usually done and the children are on their own. They try to turn themselves in to the migra, or Border Patrol, as soon as possible. They know their best bet is to be formally detained by Border Patrol officers: crossing the desert beyond the border alone is too dangerous, if not impossible. They also know that if they are not caught at this point, or if they do not surrender themselves to the law, it is unlikely that they will arrive at their final destination—the home of a relative in some city, usually far from the border. If the legal proceedings don't begin now, their fate will be to remain undocumented, like many of their parents or adult relatives already in the United States. Life as an undocumented migrant is perhaps not worse than the life they are fleeing, but it is certainly not the life that anyone wants. So, the children who cross the border, into the desert, try to stick to the busier roads and walk openly along highways, until someone—hopefully an officer and not a vigilante—sees them.

I remember a teenager who, during an interview in court, told me of his increasing desperation when, after hours of walking the arid plains of New Mexico, the Border Patrol still hadn't appeared. It was not until his second day of walking in the desert under the burning sun that a vehicle finally appeared on the far horizon. He stood in the middle of the road, waving his arms. And when the vehicle pulled over beside him, to his immense relief, two tall officers stepped out and detained him.

My mom always told me I was born under a lucky star, he said when he finished his story.

As soon as a child is in the custody of Border Patrol officials, he or she is placed in a detention center, commonly known as the hielera, or the "icebox." The icebox derives its name from the fact that the children in it are under ICE (Immigration and Customs Enforcement)

21

custody. The name also points out the fact that the detention centers along the border are a kind of enormous refrigerator for people, constantly blasted with gelid air as if to ensure that the foreign meat doesn't go bad too quickly—naturally, it must be harboring all sorts of deadly germs. The children are treated more like carriers of diseases than children. In July 2015, for example, the American Immigration Lawyers Association (AILA) filed a complaint after learning that in a detention center in Dilley, Texas, 250 children were mistakenly given adult-strength hepatitis A vaccinations. The children became gravely ill and had to be hospitalized.

By law, the maximum time a person can remain in the icebox is seventy-two hours, but children are often kept for longer, subject not only to the inhumane conditions and frigid temperatures but also to verbal and physical mistreatment. They sometimes have nowhere to lie down to sleep, are not allowed to use the bathrooms as frequently as they need to, and are underfed.

They only give out frozen sandwiches twice a day there, another teenager I once screened told me.

That's all you ate? I asked.

No, not me.

What do you mean, not you?

I didn't eat those things.

Why not?

Because they give belly-sadness.

As we drive from southwestern New Mexico toward Arizona, it becomes more and more difficult to ignore the uncomfortable irony of it: we are traveling in the direction opposite the children whose stories we are now following so closely. As we get closer to the border and begin taking back roads, we do not see a single migrant—child or adult. We see other things, though, that indicate their ghostly presence, past or future. Along the narrow dirt road in New Mexico that goes from a ghost town called Shakespeare to another town called Animas we see a trail of flags that volunteer groups tie to trees or fences, indicating that there are tanks filled with water there for people to drink as they cross the desert. Occasionally, we are overtaken by big pickup trucks, and it's hard not to imagine the men behind their steering wheels: big men with beards or shaved heads or abundant tattoos; vigilant, patriotic men who carry pistols and rifles by constitutional right and feel entitled to use them if they see a group of *aliens* walking in the desert. As we approach Animas, we also begin to see fleeting herds of Border Patrol cars like ominous white stallions racing toward the horizon.

We decide not to tell anyone in diners and gas stations that we are Mexican, just in case. But we are stopped a few times by Border Patrol officials and have to show our passports and display big smiles when we explain we are just writers and just on vacation. We have to confirm that yes, we are only writers, even if yes, we are also

Mexican. Why are we there and what are we writing—
they always want to know.

We are writing a Western, sir.

That's what we tell them, that we are writing a
Western. We also tell them we came to Arizona for
the open skies and the silence and the emptiness—this
second part, more true than the part about writing the
Western, which is untrue. Handing back our passports,
one official says sardonically:

So you come all the way down here for *the
inspiration.*

We know better than to contradict anyone who
carries a badge and a gun, so we just say:

Yes, sir.

Because—how do you explain that it is never
inspiration that drives you to tell a story, but rather a
combination of anger and clarity? How do you say: No,
we do not find inspiration here, but we find a country
that is as beautiful as it is broken, and we are somehow
now part of it, so we are also broken with it, and feel
ashamed, confused, and sometimes hopeless, and are
trying to figure out how to do something about all that.

We roll the windows up and keep driving. To dis-
tract ourselves from the aftertaste of the Border Patrol
encounter, I look for a playlist and press Shuffle. One
song that often pops up is "Straight to Hell" by the
Clash. We didn't suspect that that song would become a

kind of leitmotif of our trip. Who would have known that a song partly about the post-Vietnam War "Amerasian" children and their exclusion from the American Dream would become, forty years later, a song about Central American children in the American Nightmare. These icy lines give me *belly-sadness:*

> In no-man's-land
> There ain't no asylum here
> King Solomon he never lived 'round here.

Question seven on the questionnaire is "Did anything happen on your trip to the U.S. that scared you or hurt you?" The children seldom give details of their experiences along the journey through Mexico upon a first screening, and it's not necessarily useful to push them for more information. What happens to them between their home countries and their arrival in the United States can't always help their defense before an immigration judge, so the question doesn't make up a substantial part of the interview. But, as a Mexican, this is the question I feel most ashamed of, because what happens to children during their journey through Mexico is always worse than what happens anywhere else.

The numbers tell horror stories.

Rapes: eighty percent of the women and girls who cross Mexico to get to the U.S. border are raped on the way. The situation is so common that most of them take contraceptive precautions as they begin the journey north.

Abductions: in 2011, the National Human Rights Commission in Mexico published a special report on immigrant abductions and kidnappings, revealing that the number of abduction victims between April and September 2010—a period of just six months—was 11,333.

Deaths and disappearances: though it's impossible to establish an actual number, some sources estimate that, since 2006, around 120,000 migrants have disappeared in their transit through Mexico.

Beyond the terrifying but abstract statistics, many horror stories have recently tattooed themselves in the collective social conscience in Mexico. One specific story, though, became a turning point. On August 24, 2010, the bodies of seventy-two Central and South American migrants were found, piled up in a mass grave, at a ranch in San Fernando, Tamaulipas. Some had been tortured, and all had been shot in the back of the head. Three migrants in the group had faked their deaths and, though wounded, survived. They lived to tell the complete story: members of the drug cartel Los Zetas had perpetrated the mass murder after the migrants had refused to work for them and did not have the means to pay a ransom.

I remember the dark days when this news broke out in Mexico—thousands or perhaps millions of people in front of newspapers, radios, and TV screens, all of them asking: How? Why? What did we do? Where did we go wrong, as a society, to make something like this possible? Even now, we don't know the answer. No one does. What we do know is that, since then, hundreds of additional mass graves have been discovered. Every month, every week, they continue to be discovered. And even though the story of "Los 72"—the seventy-two men and women, girls and boys, all brutally murdered—changed the way in which both Mexican society and the rest of the world views the situation of migrants crossing Mexican territory, nothing has actually been done about it.

There are, of course, some redeeming stories in Mexico. There is the story of Las Patronas, the group of women in Veracruz who, years ago, started throwing bottled water and food to the migrants aboard La Bestia and are now a formal humanitarian group. There are also the many shelters that offer food and refuge to migrants as they travel through Mexico, the most well-known of which is Hermanos en el Camino, run by Father Alejandro Solalinde. But these stories—small oases in the no-man's-land Mexico has become—are only exceptions. If anything, they are fleeting glints of hope in the dark and raucous nightmare where the metal wheels of La Bestia continually screech and howl.

So when I have to ask children that seventh question—"Did anything happen on your trip to the U.S. that scared you or hurt you?"—all I want to do is cover my face and my ears and disappear. But I know better, or try to. I remind myself to swallow the rage, grief, and shame; remind myself to just sit still and listen closely, in case a child does happen to reveal a particular detail that can end up being key to his or her defense against deportation.

The danger migrants face in their journeys doesn't end when they finally reach the U.S.-Mexico border. Question number eight addresses crimes and rights violations in U.S. territory: "Has anyone hurt, threatened, or frightened you since you came to the U.S.?"

There are many stories about such violations. Some are liminal, like the well-known case of a sixteen-year-old boy on the Mexican side of the border who, in 2012, was shot to death by an American officer on the U.S. side who later claimed the boy and other people had thrown rocks at him. The officer argued self-defense: his bullets for their rocks. And the dangers continue once the border is crossed. We know, for instance, that civilian vigilantes and owners of private ranches go out to hunt undocumented migrants, either as a matter of conviction or merely for sport.

Many migrants also die of dehydration, hunger, or accidents. At the forensic institute of Pima County, Arizona, alone, more than 2,200 human remains have been registered since 2001, the majority of which are still unidentified. The area surrounding the border between Mexico and the United States is a big common grave, and the migrants who die in this portion of our continent become no more than "bones in the desert"—as Sergio González Rodríguez once said about the many women murdered in and around Ciudad Juárez during the peak of the femicide crisis, perhaps also foreshadowing the destiny of many more people. It is almost impossible to identify human remains recovered from the desert, as they are frequently discovered in a very advanced state of decomposition and the lines of communication between family members looking for their missing and the institutions responsible for the remains are limited, if not completely absent. One notable effort to counter this desolating map of current and future anonymous dead was organized by the nonprofit Humane Borders, which, among other important work, created an online search mechanism that matches names of deceased migrants to the specific geographical coordinates in the desert where their remains were found. That way, family members of the missing can type a name into a search bar and either confirm their worst fears, when the map zooms in on a red dot in the desert, or continue to wait and hope. Writer and former Border Patrol officer Francisco Cantú has written poignantly about these death maps and all the "clearly marked ghosts" that dot the wide deserts in the southern United States.

Numbers and maps tell horror stories, but the stories of deepest horror are perhaps those for which there are no numbers, no maps, no possible accountability, no words ever written or spoken. And perhaps the only way to grant any justice—were that even possible—is by hearing and recording those stories over and over again so that they come back, always, to haunt and shame us. Because being aware of what is happening in our era and choosing to do nothing about it has become unacceptable. Because we cannot allow ourselves to go on normalizing horror and violence. Because we can all be held accountable if something happens under our noses and we don't dare even look.

We returned to Manhattan at the end of the summer of 2014. The family's green cards were waiting for us in a stack of mail piled high by the door—all of them except mine. My stepson went back to Mexico, my daughter went back to school, my husband and I went back to work, and life went back to normal—almost. I still had to figure out what to do with my lost green card, so I began to consult my lawyer regularly. We discussed possible reasons for the delay. Maybe, she suggested,

Homeland Security was doing a more thorough background check:

Do you travel to Muslim-majority countries? my lawyer asked more than once.

I had only been to Jordan and Turkey, and that was ten years before.

Are you sure?

I went to Indonesia as a girl, I remembered when, on another phone call, she repeated the question. There were other questions:

Have you been a member of any organization that represents a threat to the United States?

My answer was probably boring:

I'm a veteran member of the United World Colleges and a recent member of both the Modern Language Association and the Association of Writers and Writing Programs—congregations of nerds, basically, with a certain enthusiasm for education, academics, and literature.

Her questions seemed increasingly unreasonable and bizarre. But we had to come up with plans B and C, so I complied and answered, filed more petitions, and spent endless hours on the customer service line for the U.S. Citizenship and Immigration Services (USCIS). We had already applied for temporary work permits, which came in the mail a few months later. But there was still no sign of my green card. We looked for other solutions until, one day, my lawyer told me she had to hand my case over to someone else because she had just been offered a job at a nonprofit organization, working on cases defending child migrants, and had to give up her private practice.

Ever since I was left somewhat alone, without gods, I have been a ferocious believer in the power of small coincidences. That is how chance works, at least for those of us who do not have the certainty of grander schemes. It was thanks to my lost green card, and thanks to my lawyer abandoning my case, that I became involved with a much more urgent problem. My more trivial pursuits as an "alien writer" or "pending Mexican" took me into the heart of something larger and more important.

As I walked down Broadway one morning, speaking to my lawyer over the phone one last time before she handed off my case, I inquired about her new job. She explained that the Obama administration had decided to create a priority juvenile docket in immigration courts to deal with the deportation proceedings of thousands of undocumented children. Suddenly, with the surge of arrivals, there was an urgent demand for lawyers in the immigration courts, and thus, she had been offered this new position. Since the majority of lawyers were monolingual, she explained, there was a special need for lawyers who, like her, spoke Spanish. Before we hung up, I asked if there was a need for translators or interpreters in court, even if they weren't lawyers, and she said of course there was. I still had questions as we hung up, but not the right words to articulate them at that moment: What was the priority juvenile docket? Who was defending these children, and who was accusing them? And of what crime, exactly?

She put me in touch with a lawyer from the American Immigration Lawyers Association that same day.

II

COURT

I started working as an interpreter in the New York immigration court in March 2015. I convinced my nineteen-year-old niece to come with me, at least for the first day. She had just moved to New York, was living with us, and was waiting for her college application results. Her life was—as it should be for anyone at that point—a wild and beautiful mess.

On our first day of work, my niece and I took the subway downtown in the early morning and walked to the big, ominous building at 26 Federal Plaza. The security procedures to enter the building are a little like the ones at an airport: you have to show your passport; take off your jackets, scarves, and shoes; deposit your bags on an inspection belt; and go through a metal detector monitored by police.

Inside, the building branches vertically and horizontally into hallways, offices, windows, courtrooms, and waiting rooms. There are few signs and few people you can ask for assistance or directions, so it's easy to get lost. The building's labyrinthine architecture is, in a way, a replica of the u.s. immigration system. And, as in any labyrinth, some find their way out and some don't. Those who don't might remain there forever, invisible specters who go up and down elevators and wander the hallways, imprisoned in circular nightmares.

A lawyer from the AILA whom I had contacted by phone a few months earlier met us on the ground floor of the building. She led us to the eleventh floor, and there she introduced us to two lawyers from The Door—a Manhattan-based nonprofit that provides kids and teenagers with services ranging from legal assistance to counseling to English and hip-hop classes— with whom we would be working that day and over the following months.

After the official introductions, the lawyers from The Door asked us to wait for a while in the little room adjacent to the one where the interviews are conducted. We had arrived too early; they hadn't finished planning the agenda for the day, and no children had shown up yet. I picked a chair in the waiting room, and my niece went to peek into the screening room where the lawyers were preparing, through the door left ajar. She promptly returned to report—with pride and enthusiasm in keeping with her age—that all the staff members from The Door were young women. I responded with a stoic nod, perhaps in an effort to display more fortitude and aplomb than I have, to appear neither moved by her comment nor frightened by what awaited us on the other side of the door.

Soon after, the lawyers let us into the screening room, where they outlined the procedure we would follow. The plan on that first day was for each of us to shadow a lawyer, learning how to use the intake questionnaire and how to conduct the interviews. Once we were familiar with the process, we would interview the children directly, without a lawyer. But so many children showed up that morning that the lawyers decided to hand us packets with copies of the intake questionnaire, and trust that we'd do the job well on our own. We had no idea what we were doing; no idea of the depth and magnitude of what we were dealing with.

Between the summer of 2014 and the first months of 2015, when my niece and I began working in court, constant coverage of the children's crisis had slowly made the general picture a little clearer for everyone who followed the news.

This much, at least, became clear. Most children came from Guatemala, El Salvador, and Honduras—the three countries that make up the Northern Triangle—and practically all of them were fleeing gang violence. Although the flow of youths migrating alone to the United States from these territories had been observed for years, there had been a considerable and sudden increase in the numbers. From October 2013 to the moment the crisis was declared in June 2014, the total number of child migrants detained at the border approached 80,000. This sudden increase set off alarms in the United States and provoked the declaration of the crisis. (Later, in the summer of 2015, it became known that between April 2014 and August 2015, more than 102,000 unaccompanied children had been detained at the border.)

The room where screenings are conducted in the New York immigration court feels improvised, like a small refugee camp occupied temporarily by local organizations and the children they screen tirelessly, every day. The space resembles a church: a rectangle, vast and austere, furnished only with benches lined up one after another. At its front, a wooden balustrade with a little door in the center cordons off an area with two large mahogany tables at which the children, lawyers, and interpreters sit for the interviews. Crayons and pads of paper are set out at the ends of the tables to entertain the younger children. During each interview, the child's relatives sit on the benches on the other side of the balustrade and wait, like spectators in a silent mass. It's against protocol for relatives to join the children during the interviews, since their presence could influence the answers they give. Against the walls of the room, instead of the statues of saints or paintings that would decorate a church, are moveable chalkboards on which lawyers and interpreters make notes and children draw and scribble while they wait their turn.

We didn't quite grasp the bigger picture during our first hours in court conducting screenings. Blindly, we simply followed all the questions on the intake questionnaire, one by one, and translated the answers. What we were really doing there that morning was providing backup for organizations dealing with an emergency. Not the emergency at the border, detonated with the surge of arrivals, but the quieter, more bureaucratic, legal emergency created by the federal government's decision to create a priority juvenile docket in response to that surge.

Before the immigration crisis was declared in the summer of 2014, minors seeking immigration relief were given approximately twelve months to find a lawyer to represent their case before their first court hearing. But when the crisis was declared and Obama's administration created the priority juvenile docket, that window was reduced to twenty-one days. In real and practical terms, what the creation of that priority docket meant was that the cases involving unaccompanied minors from Central America were grouped together and moved to the top of the list of pending cases in immigration court. Being moved to the top of a list, in this context, was the least desirable thing—at least from the point of view of the children involved. Basically, the priority juvenile docket implied that deportation proceedings against them were accelerated by 94 percent, and that both they and the organizations that normally provided legal representation now had much less time to build a defense.

Nonprofit organizations around the country reacted immediately when they heard about the priority juvenile docket. In New York, for example, as early as August 2014, some organizations got together and decided to form an emergency coalition, called the Immigrant Children Advocates' Relief Effort (ICARE). There were seven organizations in that coalition—the Legal Aid Society, The Door, Catholic Charities, Central American Legal Assistance, Make the Road New York, Safe Passage, and Kids in Need of Defense—and together they joined efforts to figure out a way to respond quickly and well to the docket. It was they who put together the questions on the intake questionnaire that my niece and I, along with other volunteers, would be using while we conducted our interviews.

Ever since the priority docket was created, children are being (and will continue to be) deported in much greater numbers and at a much faster rate. Many children, though they should be given an equal right to due process, are being deported before they can even find lawyers who will take on their cases. What child can find a lawyer in twenty-one days? And though nonprofits reacted quickly and worked together to create a screening questionnaire that would channel children's cases as quickly as possible to legal representatives, they are understaffed and working against a ticking clock. How can a handful of organizations come up with a good plan to defend all those cases, given such little time?

The priority juvenile docket, in sum, was the government's coldest, cruelest possible answer to the arrival of refugee children. Ethically, that answer was more than questionable. In legal terms, it was a kind of backdoor escape route to avoid dealing with an impending reality suddenly knocking at the country's front doors.

During a short break that first morning, my niece pointed out a chalkboard pushed up against one of the walls in the screening room. On it someone had made a list of words, divided into four categories. We reviewed it together.

> Border: coyote, migration police, icebox, shelter
> Court: The Door & other organizations, lawyers
> Home: family, guardians
> Community: ???

The words were written in Spanish. To me they read like an inscrutable haiku. I don't know what my niece made of the list, but she copied everything down in a little notebook. I wasn't carrying a notebook. Later that morning, one of the lawyers explained that the list was there to help children recall the phases of their journey during the interview. She didn't say, but in some way, we understood that the words scribbled on the board were also a kind of scaffolding holding all of those broken stories together.

I recall every nuance of the first story I heard and translated in court. Perhaps only because it was the story of a boy I encountered again, a few months later, and have ever since kept in close contact with. Or perhaps because it's a story condensed in a very specific, material detail that has continued to haunt me: a piece of paper that the boy pulled from his pocket toward the end of his interview, the creases and edges worn. He unfolded it gently, slowly, treated it with the same careful precision a surgeon might have when making a decisive incision. He laid it in front of me on the table. As I skimmed through it, still unsure about what he was showing me, he explained that the document was a copy of a police report he'd filed more than a year and a half ago. The report stated, in three or four typewritten sentences, all in capital letters and with some grammatical mistakes, that the subject in question raised a complaint against gang members who waited for him outside of his high school every day, frequently followed him home, and began threatening to kill him. It ended with the vague promise to "investigate" the situation. After showing it to me, he folded the document back up and put it in his pants pocket, rubbing his palm now and then against the denim, like he was activating a lucky charm.

When our first day of work in court was over, my niece and I took the A train back home. As our subway sped uptown, along dark tunnels, through stations, past ghostly strangers waiting on platforms, the image of that piece of paper came back to me, insistently, with the strange power of symbols. It was just a piece of paper, damp with sweat, eroded by friction, folded and tucked inside a boy's pocket. Originally, it had been a legal document, a complaint filed by a boy hoping to produce a change in his life. Now it was more of a historical document that disclosed the failure of the document's original purpose and also explained the boy's decision to leave that life. In a less obvious but equally material way, the document was also a road map of a migration, a testimony of the five thousand miles it traveled inside a boy's pocket, aboard trains, on foot, in trucks, across various national borders, all the way to an immigration court in a distant city, where it was finally unfolded, spread out on a mahogany table, and read out loud by a stranger who had to ask that boy: Why did you come to the United States?

News coverage of the immigration crisis eventually provided a general map, and more precise numbers about its magnitude, but it did not clarify its deeper causes and consequences. It did not answer *why*. The very notion of this "immigration crisis" referred only to the sudden surge in arrivals of Central American children to the United States. From the beginning, the crisis was viewed as an institutional hindrance, a problem that Homeland Security was "suffering" and that Congress and immigration judges had to solve. Few narratives have made the effort to turn things around and understand the crisis from the point of view of the children involved. The political response to the crisis, therefore, has always centered on one question, which is more or less: What do we do with all these children now? Or, in blunter terms: How do we get rid of them or dissuade them from coming?

Questions nine, ten, and eleven on the intake questionnaire are: "How do you like where you're living now?"; "Are you happy here?"; "Do you feel safe?" It's hard to imagine that these children, considered a hindrance to institutions and unwanted intruders by a large part of the society to which they've just arrived, soon to face a judge and defend themselves against a removal order, indeed "like where they are living." In the media and much of the official political discourse, the word "illegal" prevails over "undocumented" and the term "immigrant" over "refugee." How would anyone who is stigmatized as an "illegal immigrant" feel "safe" and

44

"happy"? But the children usually respond yes to those three questions.

Working early-morning shifts in court and staying up late together many, many nights—watching good and bad documentaries, reading reports, discussing research papers and news articles—my niece and I slowly began to understand the crisis better, in its hemispheric proportions and historical roots. One of the questions that we dug into most consistently had to do with the gangs all the children talked about during court screenings: the Mara Salvatrucha 13 (MS-13) and the Barrio 18 (or Calle 18).

We read, read some more, discussed, and tried to make sense of all of it. Both gangs originated in Los Angeles in the 1980s, a time when the Bloods, Crips, Nazi Low Riders, and Aryan Brotherhood, among many others, were already well established in the United States. The original Barrio 18 members were second-generation Hispanics who grew up in L.A. gang culture. The MS-13 was originally a small coalition of immigrants from El Salvador who had sought exile in the U.S. during the long and ruthless Salvadoran Civil War (1979–1992), in which the military-led government relentlessly massacred left-wing opposition groups. We looked more deeply into the war and the struggle between the left-wing guerilla group Farabundo Martí National Liberation Front and the military government. The primary ally of that government, we discover (and should have predicted), was the United States. The Carter administration and, perhaps more actively, the Reagan administration funded and provided military resources to the government that massacred so many and led many others to exile. Around one-fifth of the population of El Salvador fled. Many of those who sought exile ended up as political refugees in the United States—around three hundred thousand of them in Los Angeles. The whole story is an absurd, circular nightmare.

Later on, in the 1990s, anti-immigration policies and programs in the U.S. led to massive deportations of Central Americans. Among them were thousands of MS-13 members—those perhaps quite understandably unwanted in the country. But the policies backfired: gang deportations became more of a metastasis than an eradication. Now the gang has become a kind of transnational army, with more than seventy thousand members spread across the United States, Mexico, and the Northern Triangle.

The whole thing is a mess, a puzzle impossible to piece together using common sense and logic. But this much is clear: until all the governments involved—the American, Mexican, Salvadoran, Honduran, and Guatemalan governments, at least—acknowledge their shared accountability in the roots and causes of the children's exodus, solutions to the crisis will be impossible.

Questions twelve and thirteen address some kind of concern for accountability in U.S. territory. Not the government's possible accountability for political crimes, of course—those are always robed in a cloak of invisibility or impunity, especially if they are committed abroad, and especially if "abroad" is a tiny little country in the Hispanic Americas. Rather, the questions address a concern for accountability for crimes committed on U.S. soil, in which a migrant's cooperation with the government might be generously rewarded: "Have your parents or siblings been the victim of a crime since they came to the U.S.?" and "Was it reported to the police?"

Victims of certain crimes committed in the United States, as immigration law has it, may be eligible for a form of relief known as the U visa. If granted, the U visa is a path to lawful permanent residency for both the victims and their families (i.e., the highly coveted family green card). Eligibility, however, hinges on the victim's successful cooperation with the government in the prosecution of the crime in question. The subtext of this is somewhat cynical and the terms of the barter a little unequal: We'll give you a visa for the "substantial mental and physical abuse" that you may have suffered as a result of a crime committed against you . . . *but.* Before we do, you have to agree to assisting law enforcement and government officials in the investigation and prosecution of the crime.

For victims of some crimes, real and horrible crimes, permission to stay in American territory is probably insufficient recompense. But it's better than nothing. It's certainly better than the right to a mass grave in Tamaulipas or Veracruz, for instance—the most common "permanent residence" granted to Central American migrants who travel across Mexico.

Most children arrive looking for their parents, who came to the United States years before. If not their parents, they seek refuge with relatives who have kept in close enough contact to still be reachable, relatives who may have been sending them money for years and who perhaps helped finance or plan their trip. These same relatives are the ones who usually receive the children if they're able to cross the border without being deported, and once they have the children in custody, they can declare themselves legal guardians.

The next questions open a window into how the migration of children is reorganizing and redefining the traditional family structure.

Fourteen, fifteen, and sixteen are about the child's relationship with family members who stayed behind: "Do you still have any family members that live in your home country?"; "Are you in touch with anyone in your home country?"; "Who/how often?" The family tree of migrant families is always split into two trunks: those who leave and those who stay. The ones who usually stay behind are the youngest and the eldest, though children as young as one or two, and some even younger who traveled in the arms of slightly older siblings or cousins, have shown up in court. The ones who leave are usually the oldest children and the teenagers, following the adult relatives who went before.

Seventeen and eighteen refer to family members who might act as sponsors, or the people under whose care the children might now live: "Do you have any other close family members who live in the u.s.?"; "Immigration status?" The immigration status of family members is almost always "undocumented." This, of course, means that presenting themselves in court in the company of a sponsor exposes other members of their family to a system that they have been dodging, sometimes for decades. This guilt weighs on some children noticeably. Many ask during their interviews if their guardians will now be at risk for deportation. The new situation creates tensions and complications within families. Sponsors have to give all their details when the children are screened, from their names to their exact addresses. They suddenly find themselves in a position of utter vulnerability. And yet thousands of children and their sponsors have presented themselves in court since the surge began. The states with the highest number of children released to sponsors since the crisis was declared are Texas (over

10,000 children), California (almost 9,000 children), and New York (over 8,000 children).

Nineteen, twenty, and twenty-one, on the other hand, refer to the family members the child lived with before arriving in the United States: "Who did you live with in your home country?"; "Did you ever live with anyone else?"; "How did you get along with the people with whom you lived?" The children's answers vary, and it's almost always necessary to reformulate the questions and ask them again, because upon entering the country many prefer not to speak of the familial situations they are fleeing, either to avoid the pain and humiliation they entail or out of loyalty. But in many answers, it can be inferred that "the people with whom you lived" are precisely the reason the child was driven out of his or her home and community in the first place.

And finally, question number twenty-two addresses the very nucleus of a family unit: "Did you stay in touch with your parents?" Most children give the same answer:

No.

No, they say, they did not keep in touch and have no idea where their parents are. Others didn't keep in touch for years but then were, suddenly, living with them again: familial reunification of absolute strangers.

As the months go by I interview dozens of children. The stories they tell me bleed into each other, get confused with one another, shuffle and mix. Maybe it's because, though each story is different, they all come together easily, pieces of a larger puzzle. Each child comes from a different place, a separate life, a distinct set of experiences, but their stories usually follow the same predictable, fucked-up plot.

Which goes more or less as follows: Children leave their homes with a coyote. They cross Mexico in the hands of this coyote, riding La Bestia. They try not to fall into the hands of rapists, corrupt police-men, murderous soldiers, and drug gangs who might enslave them in poppy or marijuana fields, if they don't shoot them in the head and mass-bury them. If something goes wrong, and something happens to a child, the coyote is not held accountable. In fact, no one is ever held accountable. The children who make it all the way to the U.S. border turn themselves in to Border Patrol officers and are formally detained. (Often by officers who say things like "Speak English! Now you're in America!") They are then placed in the icebox. And, later, in a temporary shelter. There they must start looking for their parents—if they have parents—or for relatives who will sponsor them. Later, they are sent to wherever their sponsor lives. And finally, they have to appear in court, where they can defend themselves against deportation—if they have a lawyer.

There is one exception, however, one little twist to the part of the plot where children are formally detained by Border Patrol officers. The exception is: being Mexican. Mexican children detained by Border Patrol can be deported back immediately. They don't have to be given temporary shelter, are not allowed to attempt contact with parents or relatives in the U.S., and are certainly not granted a right to a formal hearing in court where they could defend themselves, legally, against a deportation order.

If a Border Patrol officer, upon detaining and screening a Mexican child, determines that this child (1) is not a victim of a severe form of trafficking in persons, (2) is not at risk of trafficking upon return, (3) does not have a "credible fear" of persecution, and (4) is able to make an independent decision about returning, then the officer is entitled to deport the child. A Border Patrol officer can base a decision to deport a Mexican child on any evidence—no matter how substantial or insubstantial—and is not required to document a rationale behind it.

The procedure by which Mexican children are deported in this way is called "voluntary return." And, as unbelievable as it may seem, voluntary return is the most common verdict. Other than a handful of lucky exceptions, all Mexican children are deported under this procedure. This—irrational, if not completely absurd—practice is legally backed by an amendment to the Trafficking Victims Protection Reauthorization Act, which was signed by President G. W. Bush in 2008. The amendment states that children from countries that share borders with the U.S. can be deported without formal immigration proceedings. That is, if a child comes from either Mexico or Canada, he or she is immediately "deportable"—a "removable alien." This amendment was Bush's last gift to American immigration law in his vast legacy of chingaderas, in urban Mexican slang, or nasty-shitty policies, in approximate English translation.

III

HOME

Often, my daughter asks me:

So, how does the story of those children end?

I don't know how it ends yet, I usually say.

My daughter often follows up on the stories she half-hears. There is one story that obsesses her, a story I only tell her in pieces and for which I have not yet been able to offer a real ending. It begins with two girls in the courtroom. They're five and seven years old, and they're from a small village in Guatemala. Spanish is their second language, but the older girl speaks it well. We sit around the mahogany table in the room where the interviews take place, and their mother observes from one of the benches in the back. The little girl concentrates on her coloring book, a crayon in her right hand. The older one has her hands crossed as an adult might, and she answers my questions one by one. She is a little shy but tries to be clear and precise in her answers, delivering all of them with a big smile, toothless here and there.

Why did you come to the United States?

I don't know.

How did you travel here?

A man brought us.

A coyote?

No, a man.

Was he nice to you?

Yes, he was nice, I think.

And where did you cross the border?

I don't know.

Texas? Arizona?

Yes! Texas Arizona.

I realize it's impossible to go on with the interview, so I ask the lawyers to make an exception and allow the mother to meet with us, at least for a while. We go back to question one, and the mother responds for the girls, filling holes, explaining things, and also telling her own version of the story.

When the younger of her daughters turned two, she decided to migrate north and left them in the care of their grandmother. She crossed two national borders with no documents. She wasn't detained by Border Patrol and managed to cross the desert with a group of people. After a few weeks she arrived in Long Island, where she had a cousin. That's where she settled. Years passed, and the girls grew up. Years passed, and she remarried. She had another child.

One day she called her mother—the grandmother of the girls—and told her that the time had come: she had saved enough money to bring the girls over. I don't know how the grandmother responded to the news of her granddaughters' imminent departure, but she noted the instructions down carefully and later explained them to the girls: in a few days, a man was going to come for them, a man who would help them get back to their mother. She told them that it would be a long trip, but that he would keep them safe. The man had taken many other girls from their village safely across the two borders to their mothers, and everything had gone well. So everything would go well this time, too.

The day before they left, their grandmother sewed a ten-digit telephone number on the collars of the dress each girl would wear throughout the entire trip. It was a ten-digit number the girls had not been able to memorize, as hard as she tried to get them to, so she had decided to embroider it on their dresses and repeat, over and over, a single instruction: they should never take this dress off, not even to sleep, and as soon as they reached America, as soon as they met the first American policeman, they were to show the inside of the dress's collar to him. He would then dial the number and let them speak to their mother. The rest would follow.

The rest did follow: they made it to the border, were kept in custody, in the hielera, for an indefinite time period (they didn't remember how many days, but they said that they were colder there than they had ever been). After that they went to a shelter, and a few weeks later they were put on a plane and flown to JFK, where their mother, baby brother, and stepfather were waiting for them.

That's it? my daughter asks.

That's it, I tell her.

That's how it ends?

Yes, that's how it ends.

But of course it doesn't end there. That's just where it begins, with a court summons: a first Notice to Appear.

Once children receive a Notice to Appear, they have to present themselves in immigration court. If they don't show up (because they fear going to court, or perhaps because they have since moved, or because they simply didn't get the notice) they are usually "removed in absentia." An immigration judge, assisted by a translator, informs the ones who do show up that they have the right to an attorney, but at no expense to the U.S. government. In other words, it is the children's responsibility to find and pay for a lawyer, or find a free lawyer, who can help them defend their case against the U.S. government attorney seeking to deport them.

A typical immigration hearing begins with the judge stating the basic facts:

This is September 15, 2014, New York, state of New York. This is Immigration Judge [name of judge].

This is in the matter of [name of the child respondent].

Then come questions directed at the respondent (the child), such as if he or she responds to Spanish, if he or she is enrolled in school, and whether he or she lives at the given address. Then the judge states that he or she will be speaking to the attorney and asks:

How do you plead?

We admit the allegations and concede the charge.

And what is the charge? Fundamentally, that the child came to the United States without lawful permission and is therefore "removable." Admitting this charge alone leads to deportation unless the child's attorney can find those potential avenues of relief that form a defense against it. The admission of guilt, then, is a kind of door that the law holds half open. It is the only way for the accused to begin defending themselves against a categorical sentence and seek legal avenues to immigration relief.

The most common forms of immigration relief are asylum and special immigrant juvenile (SIJ) status. If the child is eligible for either of these, he or she may remain in the United States legally and can later apply for lawful permanent residency and even citizenship.

Usually, the kind of harm the children are fleeing makes them eligible for asylum or SIJ status. This status can be obtained in two steps. First, a family court must determine that they are impeded from reunification with at least one of their parents because of abuse, abandonment, neglect, or a similar basis under state law, and that reunification or return to their home country is not in their best interest. Once the family court makes this ruling, the minor can request sɪj status in the immigration court.

Asylum, on the other hand, is granted to people who are fleeing persecution (or who have a fear of future persecution) based on their race, religion, nationality, political opinion, and/or association with a particular social group. It is very difficult to be granted asylum because it is not enough that these children have suffered unspeakable harm, that they will continue to fall victim to the systematic and targeted violence of criminal groups. The harm or persecution must be proved to be *because of* at least one of those four classifications. The main problem with asylum—the reason lawyers often consider it a secondary choice—is that if it's granted, the children can never return to their home country, where they fear being persecuted, without jeopardizing their immigration status in the United States. Less common are the U visa, which can only be granted to victims of certain crimes, and the T visa, for victims of human trafficking.

If the child answers the questionnaire "correctly," he or she is more likely to have a case strong enough to increase its chances of being placed with a pro bono attorney. An answer is "correct" if it strengthens the child's case and provides a potential avenue of relief. So, in the warped world of immigration, a correct answer is when, for example, a girl reveals that her father is an alcoholic who physically or sexually abused her, or when a boy reports that he received death threats or that he was beaten repeatedly by several gang members after refusing to acquiesce to recruitment at school and has the physical injuries to prove it. Such answers—more common than exceptional—may open doors to potential immigration relief and, eventually, legal status in the United States. When children don't have enough battle wounds to show, they may not have any way to successfully defend their cases and will most likely be "removed" back to their home country, often without a trial.

The interpreters have no control over the type of legal assistance a child receives. We listen to their stories in Spanish and note key points in English. We must simultaneously pay close attention to the details and find ways to distribute them into categories. On the one hand, it's important to record even the most minor details from each story because a good lawyer can use them to strengthen a case in ways that might not have been evident to an interpreter. On the other, although it's not in the protocol, we often look for more general categories for each story that may tip the legal scale in favor of the future client in a future trial—categories such as "abandonment," "prostitution," "sex trafficking," "gang violence," and "death threats." But we cannot make up the answers in their favor, nor can we lead the children to tell us what is best for their cases, as much as we would like to. It can be confusing and bewildering, and I find myself not knowing where translation ends and interpretation starts.

During the interviews, I sometimes note the children's answers in the first person and sometimes in the third:

> I crossed the border by foot.
> She swam across the river.
> He comes from San Pedro Sula.
> She comes from Tegucigalpa.
> She comes from Guatemala City.
> He has not ever met his father.
> Yes I have met my mother.
> But she doesn't remember the last time she saw her.
> He doesn't know if she abandoned him.
> She sent money every month.
> No, my father didn't send money at all.

I worked in the fields, ten or maybe fifteen hours a day.

The MS-13 shot my sister. She died.

Yes, my uncle hit me often.

No, my grandmother never hit us.

As predictable as the answers start to become after months of conducting the interviews, no one is ever prepared for hearing them.

If the children are very young, in addition to translating from one language to another, the interpreters have to reconfigure the questions, shift them from the language of adults to the language of children. When I interviewed the girls with the dresses, for example, I had to break many of the intake questions up into simpler, shorter phrasings, until I was finally able to find a bridge to communicate with them. Question twenty-two, for example—"Did you stay in touch with your parents"—went through various iterations:

When you were there, how did you contact your mother?

What?

Did you talk to your mother when she was here and you were there?

Back where?

Did you mother call you on the phone?

Finally, she nodded, looking at me in silence. Then she searched for her mother's eyes, found them, and smiled. She relaxed a little and began to speak.

Yes, she told me. She had talked to her mother on the phone, and her mother had told them stories about snowstorms, and big avenues, and traffic jams, and later, stories about her new husband and their new baby brother. After that, we asked her mother to return to the area reserved for relatives of the children.

Questions twenty-three through twenty-six are a little less complicated, though redundant, and the girl was able to respond to them less hesitantly:

Twenty-three: Did you go to school in your country of origin?

Did you go to school in Guatemala?

No.

Twenty-four: How old were you when you started going to school?

I didn't go to school.

Twenty-five: When did you stop going to school?

I already told you, I never went!

Twenty-six: Why not?

I don't know.

I didn't know how to ask questions twenty-seven, twenty-eight, and twenty-nine: "Did you work in your home country?"; "What sort of work did you do?"; "How many hours did you work each day?" But I knew that

I had to find a way to do it. We were already halfway through the questionnaire, and I still didn't feel sure that a lawyer would take on the case. I reworded, translated, interpreted:

What kinds of things did you do when you lived with your grandmother?

We played.

But besides playing?

Nothing.

Did you work?

Yes.

What did you do?

I don't remember.

I went on to questions thirty, thirty-one, thirty-two, and thirty-three. The older girl answered them while the little one undressed a crayon and scratched its trunk with her fingernail.

Did you ever get in trouble at home when you lived in your home country?

No.

Were you punished if you did something wrong?

No.

How often were you punished?

Never.

Did you or anyone in your family have an illness that required special attention?

What?

The girl's answers weren't really working. They weren't working in their favor, that is. What I needed to hear, though I didn't want to hear it, was that they had been doing hard labor, labor that put their safety and integrity in danger; that they were being exploited, abused, punished, maybe threatened with death by gangs. If their answers didn't align with what the law considers reason enough for the right to protection, the only possible ending to their story was going to be a deportation order. It was going to be very hard, with the answers I was getting, to even find them a lawyer willing to take their case. The girls were so young, and even if they had a story that secured legal intervention in their favor, they didn't know the words necessary to tell it. For children of that age, telling a story—in a second language, translated to a third—a round and convincing story that successfully inserts them into legal proceedings working up to their defense, is practically impossible.

But how does the story about those girls end? my daughter asks.

I don't know how it ends, I say.

She comes back to this question often, demanding a proper conclusion with the insistence of very small children:

But what happens next, Mamma?

I don't know.

After a few months of working with The Door in court cases like this one, feelings of frustration and defeat began to settle over my niece and me. The numbers weren't adding up. There were so many more children awaiting interviews than there were interpreters and lawyers to conduct them. The ones we had interviewed now faced a shrinking window of time to find legal representation. It was clear that our only role in the court was to serve as a fragile and slippery bridge between the children and the court system. We could translate their cases, but we couldn't do anything to help them. It was like watching a child crossing a busy avenue, about to be run down by any of the many speeding cars and trucks, the two of us powerless to stop it, our hands and feet tied. One day, while we were walking to the train station, my niece said:

You know, I think I'm going to major in law instead of social work.

Why law? I asked.

My question was unnecessary. I already knew the answer. It's lawyers that are desperately needed. According to a comprehensive report issued in October 2015 by the Migration Policy Institute, the majority of children who find a lawyer do appear in court and are granted some form of relief. All the others are deported, either in absentia or in person. What is needed in particular, and urgently, are lawyers who are willing to work pro bono.

Because immigration court is a civil court, these child "aliens" are not entitled to the free legal counsel that American law guarantees to persons accused of crimes. In other words, that fourth sentence in the well-known Miranda rights—"If you cannot afford an attorney, one will be provided for you"—does not apply to them. Therefore, volunteer organizations have stepped in to do the job. Either pro bono or at very low cost, nonprofit organizations find attorneys to represent "alien" children. A handful of nonprofit organizations are responsible for all the work being done to help undocumented child migrants, and what they have accomplished is impressive. But they can provide only patchwork support, and cannot cover all the gaps.

I realize after several months of working in the court that it is better to write the children's answers in my notebook before copying them down on the intake questionnaire.

One boy says, The gang followed me after school, and I ran, with my eyes closed I ran. So I write all that down, and then, in the margin, make a note: Persecution? He says more: And they followed me to school and later they followed me home with a gun. So I write that down, too, and then make a note: Death threats? Then he says,

They kicked my door open and shot my little brother. So I write that down, too, but then I'm not sure what note to make in the margin: Home country poses life-threatening danger? Not in child's best interest to return? What words are the most precise ones? All too often I find myself not wanting to write anymore, wanting to just sit there, quietly listening, wishing that the story I'm hearing had a better ending. I listen, hoping that the bullet shot at this boy's little brother had missed. But it didn't. The little brother was killed, and the boy fled. And now he is being screened, by me. Later, his screening, like many others, is filed and sent away to a lawyer: a snapshot of a life that will wait in the dark until maybe someone finds it and decides to make it a case.

My niece and I almost always leave immigration court in silence. We leave the brutal and exceptional reality of the stories we heard and translated that day, and step into the business-as-usual reality of the city: the hum of crowded streets, the sirens, the subway's screeching when it comes to a halt. Sometimes, only sometimes, while we ride the subway back, we tell each other pieces of the stories we heard during the day. Telling stories doesn't solve anything, doesn't reassemble broken lives. But perhaps it is a way of understanding the unthinkable. If a story haunts us, we keep telling it to ourselves, replaying it in silence while we shower, while we walk alone down streets, or in our moments of insomnia.

The story that obsesses me is the first one I had to translate. It lives with me now, grows in me, all its details clear in my mind and constantly revisited. It's a story I know well and follow closely, but for which I still cannot see a possible ending.

This is how it starts. A boy and I are seated at one end of the long mahogany table. It is obvious that both of us are new to the scenario, both still uncomfortable with reducing a story to the blank spaces between questions.

First I fill in biographical information. Next to "name," "age," and "nationality," I write: Manu López, sixteen years old, Honduras. Then, next to the words "guardian," "relationship," and "current residence," I write: Alina López, aunt, 42 Port Street, Hempstead, Long Island, NY. I look at the two questions that float halfway down the page: "Where is child's mother?"; "Father?" Manu answers with a shrug, and I write: ? and ?

Why did you come to the United States?

He says nothing and looks at me, shrugs a little. I reassure him:

I'm no policewoman, I'm no official anyone, I'm not even a lawyer. I'm also not a gringa, you know? In fact, I can't help you at all. But I can't hurt you, either.

So why are *you* here then?

I'm just here to translate for you.

And what are you?

What do you mean?

I mean: where are you from?

I'm a chilanga.

Well, I'm a catracho, so we're enemies.

He's right: I'm from Mexico City and he's from Honduras, and in many ways, that makes us hostile neighbors.

Yeah, I say, but only in football, and I suck at football anyway so you've already scored five goals against me.

He smiles, perhaps almost laughs. I know he's going to let me go on with the questions. I haven't won his trust, of course, but at least I have his attention. We proceed, slowly and hesitantly. He delivers his answers in a whisper or a murmur and looks down at his clasped hands or turns around to find his aunt and baby cousin. I try to convey my words neutrally, but every question seems to either embarrass or annoy him. He answers in short sentences or with silent shrugs. No, he has never met his father. No, he did not live with his mother in his home country. He has met her, yes, but she came and went as she pleased. She liked the streets, perhaps. He doesn't like talking about her. He grew up with his grandmother, but she died last year. Everyone was dying or going north. Six months now, exactly, since she died. She used to take care of them, in Honduras, but it was his aunt, the same aunt now sitting in the back of the courtroom, who had always sent money.

How do you like living with your aunt?

He likes her. But even though she is family, he's never really known her. She has always been just a voice inside the telephone. She called regularly, from New York, to see how they were all doing. I ask who "they" are, to get a clearer picture. Or, in other words, question nineteen, with its respective branches, which in turn branch out, into always more and more complex stories:

Who did you live with in your home country?

With my grandmother and my two cousins.

How old are they?

Nineteen and thirteen. No, wait, nineteen and fourteen.

Names?

Patricia and Marta—why do you need their names?

I just do. Are the two of them still there now?

No.

So where are they?

Somewhere, on their way here.

On their way to the u.s.?

Yes.

With whom?

A coyote—who else?

Paid by?

My aunt, sitting over there.

Is she their aunt too?

No, she's their mother. If they're my cousins, she's their mother, right?

The reason for the trip that the two girls are also now making, following Manu's path, doesn't become clear to me until we finally arrive at the last ten questions. They're the most difficult to ask because they refer directly to the gangs, and it's at this point that many of the children, especially the older ones, break down. Smaller children look back at you with a mixture of bewilderment and amusement if you say "bands of organized criminals," maybe because they associate the word "bands" with musical groups. But the majority, even the littlest ones, have heard the words "ganga" or "pandillero" before, and saying them is like pressing the button on a machine that produces nightmares. Even if they don't have direct experience with the gangs, the threat lurks constantly, a monster under the bed or on the street corner—something they'll have to face sooner or later.

The teenagers have all been touched in one way or another by the tentacles of the MS-13 and Barrio 18, or other groups like them, though the degree of their contact and involvement with pandilleros varies. The teenage girls, for example, are not usually coerced into gangs

73

but are often sexually harassed by them or recruited to be girlfriends. Boys are told that their little sister, cousin, or girlfriend will be raped if they don't man up and join.

I ask Manu question thirty-four, the one that often opens Pandora's box but also gives the interviewer the most valuable material for building the minor's case: "Did you ever have trouble with gangs or crime in your home country?"

Manu tells me a confusing, fragmented story about the MS-13 and their ongoing fight against the Barrio 18. One was trying to recruit him. The other was going after him. One day some boys from Barrio 18 waited for him and his best friend outside their school. When Manu and his friend saw them there, they knew they couldn't fight. There were too many of them. He and his friend walked away, but they were followed. They tried running. They ran for a block or two, until there was a gunshot. Manu turned around—still running—and saw that his friend had fallen. More gunshots followed, but he kept running until he found an open store and went inside.

Questions thirty-five and thirty-six:

Any problems with the government in your home country? If so, what happened?

My government? Write this down in your notebook: they don't do shit for anybody like me, that's the problem.

It's then that, from his pocket, he pulls out the piece of paper that haunted me for so long—a copy of the police report he filed against the gang. He filed it months before his friend was killed, but the police never did anything. And Manu knew, because everyone knows this is how it is, that the police wouldn't do anything to prevent a second incident, or a third.

That night, after the confrontation with the gang, he called his aunt in New York. They decided he would leave the country as soon as possible. She made him promise he would not leave his house during the weeks that followed. He didn't attend his friend's funeral.

Miguel Hernández has a poem called "Elegy" about the death of a childhood friend. It's not so much a distant remembrance as an obsessive conjuring of his friend's buried corpse. These lines drive themselves into my mind the way only the sharpest images can:

> I want to gnaw at the earth with my teeth,
> I want to take the earth apart bit by bit
> with dry, burning bites.
>
> I want to mine the earth till I find you,
> and kiss your noble skull,
> and un-shroud you, and return you.

In the interview, Manu repeated twice that he wasn't at his friend's funeral. He didn't leave his house until the coyote knocked on his door and they slipped down streets of Tegucigalpa together.

His aunt paid the coyote $4,000. They left at dawn. Manu explains that boys cost $4,000 and girls $3,000.

Why?

Because boys are the worst, he says, smiling wide.

We go over the rest of the story: from Tegucigalpa to Guatemala by bus, to the Mexican border, to Arriaga and then aboard La Bestia, to the U.S.-Mexico border. No serious problems along the way, although I imagine there were serious things that don't seem serious to him anymore. From there to the icebox, the shelter, the airplane to JFK, and finally to Long Island. We're about to finish the session when he suddenly reveals an unexpected turn—the reason his two cousins, Patricia and Marta, set off on the same journey.

Why did they leave?

Something in his body language softens and becomes milder, as if the thought of his two cousins has momentarily stripped away some of his toughness— an attitude that, with practice like this, may turn into personality. When he left, he explains, the same gang that had killed his best friend started harassing his two cousins. That's when his aunt decided that she'd rather pay the $3,000 for each of her daughters and put them through the dangers of the journey than let them stay. The dangers the girls will face multiply in my head as Manu tells me all this.

Beyond the dangers posed by organized gangs and criminals in Mexico, there are also the federal, state, and municipal police forces, the army, and the immigration officials who operate under the umbrella of the Ministry of the Interior and whose roles have been reinforced by new and more severe policies. Shortly after the unaccompanied child migrant crisis was declared in the United States, and after a meeting between President Barack Obama and President Enrique Peña Nieto, the Mexican government introduced its new anti-immigration plan, the Programa Frontera Sur. The objective of the program, which was granted an initial budget of 102 million pesos from federal funds, was to halt the immigration of Central Americans through Mexico.

To justify Programa Frontera Sur, the Mexican government maintains that Mexico must protect the "safety and rights" of migrants. But the reality is something else entirely. In fact, since the program was implemented, the safety of immigrants has been compromised to an even greater extent, their lives put in a much more vulnerable situation. Anti-immigrant strategies included in the program, mostly to be implemented along the routes of La Bestia, include drones; security cameras and control centers in strategic locations (trains, tunnels, bridges, railway crossings, and city centers); fences and floodlights in the rail yards; private security teams and geolocation technology in trains; alarm systems and motion detectors on the tracks; and, last but not least, the notorious Grupos Beta, which, under the guise of a humanitarian aid organization, locates and then reports migrants to immigration officials, who can then "secure" them—a Mexican euphemism for "capture and deport." Programa Frontera Sur is the Mexican government's new augmented-reality videogame: the player who hunts down the most migrants wins.

As the Mexican government has progressively increased its hold on La Bestia, travel aboard the trains has become more and more risky and new routes have been improvised. There are now maritime routes that begin on the coasts of Chiapas, along which the migrants travel with coyotes aboard rafts and other precarious vessels. We've heard the many stories about migrants crossing the Mediterranean—that massive cemetery of a sea—so it's easy to imagine what kinds of stories we'll hear in the next few years, of migrants amid the enormous waves of the Pacific Ocean.

Since Programa Frontera Sur was launched in 2014, Mexico has massively deported Central American migrants, many of whom would have had the legal right to request asylum in either Mexico or the United States. In 2016, for example, Mexico registered the largest number of applications for asylum in recent history. That same year saw a radical increase in deportation rates of Central Americans. This of course begs the question of whether migrants' right to due process is being honored.

Most Mexicans, when asked about immigration issues, talk like they have either a PhD in Mexico-U.S. relations or direct experience with migrating illegally across the border. Mexicans are eager and tireless critics of U.S. immigration policies. And though most critiques of their northern neighbor are probably more than justified, Mexicans are far too lax and self-indulgent when it comes to evaluating our own country's immigration policies, especially where Central Americans are concerned.

Under Programa Frontera Sur, the focus of border control for the Central American exodus is shifting from the Río Grande on the U.S.-Mexico border to the Suchiate and Usumacinta Rivers on the Mexico-Guatemala border. The United States, of course, not only endorses this shift but has been generously financing it: the State Department has paid the Mexican government tens of millions of dollars to filter the migration of Central Americans. In other words, following the old tradition of Latin America–U.S. governmental relations, the Mexican government is getting paid to do the dirty work.

And President Peña Nieto—the most well-groomed, cynical, and sinister boy among the subservient Latin American bullies doing the grunt work—has earned his place as the continent's new deporter-in-chief: since 2014 he has deported more Central Americans each year than the United States, more than 150,000 in 2015. The country is now limbo for migrants, an enormous and terrifying customs office staffed as often by white-collar criminals as it is by criminals with guns and pickup trucks.

The next time I see Manu, six months later, we're in a large room on the twenty-somethingth floor of a corporate building next to South Ferry. We can see Staten Island from the window, and if we stretch our necks, we can see the Statue of Liberty. The setting is almost unreal, as if we've been thrust into a high-budget production of a Hollywood movie.

Manu is grateful, his aunt asks me to tell the three men in expensive suits who sit across from us at the lacquered table. I sense his disbelief, and perhaps he senses mine, too. The lawyers who will represent his case work for one of the most powerful and expensive corporate firms in the city. Rarely do these kinds of offices get involved in cases like this one. But thanks to the material evidence Manu has of his statements—the folded slip of paper—The Door was able to find a large firm willing to take his case pro bono. With that kind of material evidence, it would be impossible for them to lose. The lawyers at The Door transformed a dead document into legal evidence for a case.

Sometimes when cases advance to this second phase, the organizations that work in the court ask the interpreter who did the first interview to rejoin them. Since Manu's new lawyers don't speak Spanish, I was asked to continue translating for him.

I don't hesitate to show Manu my enthusiasm for our coincidental reunion in this second stage of his immigration process. I tell him about another coincidence: I'm now working at a university in Hempstead, the same city in Long Island where he lives. He receives my enthusiasm without a word, maintaining his cool. We sit around a large black table: Manu, his aunt, three lawyers, and me. We are offered coffee and snacks. Alina and I say yes to the coffee. Manu says he'll have some of everything if it's free. I translate:

Just a cookie please, thanks, that's very kind of you.

The meeting serves the sole purpose of preparing Manu's SIJ status application, though he's probably more likely eligible for asylum. We go through the lawyers' contract and then through his application. Everything runs smoothly until the lawyers ask if Manu is still enrolled in school. He is, he says. He's at Hempstead High School. But he wants to leave as soon as possible.

Why? they want to know. They remind him that if he wants to be considered for any type of formal relief, he has to be enrolled in school. He answers slowly and in a low voice, but perhaps more confidently than when I first met him in court, months ago. He looks down at his clasped hands now and again as he talks. Hempstead High School, he tells us, is a hub for MS-13 and Barrio 18. I go cold at hearing this statement, which he delivers in the tone one might use to talk about items in a supermarket. He's afraid of Barrio 18 but doesn't want to join MS-13, either, even though they are not as bad.

Suddenly, we all suspect Manu and want to ask question thirty-seven: "Have you ever been a member of a gang? Any tattoos?" No, he has no tattoos. And no, he's never been part of a gang.

Indeed, it turns out Manu has good reasons to be afraid. Members of Barrio 18 beat him up. When he tells me about this incident, he is missing his two front teeth. Showing the wide gap and trying to joke about it, he says, I used to laugh at my grandma 'cause she had no front teeth, and now I look in the mirror and I laugh at me.

After the incident with Barrio 18, his aunt Alina worried he would end up in trouble because MS-13 boys saved him from losing the rest of his teeth, and now he owes them something. When I ask him about it, he says the MS-13 in Hempstead wants him, yes, but he's not going to fall for it. He'd rather disappear than join them. Now more than ever.

What do you mean by now more than ever, Manu? I ask.

I mean now that my two cousins are here with us and I have to look out for them.

Look out for them how?

Just look out for them, 'cause Hempstead is a shit-hole full of pandilleros, just like Tegucigalpa.

Between Hempstead and Tegucigalpa there is a long chain of causes and effects. Both cities can be drawn on the same map: the map of violence related to drug trafficking. This fact is ignored, however, by almost all of the official reports. The media wouldn't put Hempstead, a city in New York, on the same plane as one in Honduras. What a scandal! Official accounts in the United States—what circulates in the newspaper or on the radio, the message from Washington, and public opinion in general—almost always locate the dividing line between "civilization" and "barbarity" just below the Río Grande.

A brief, particularly disconcerting article in the *New York Times* in October 2014 postulated a series of questions and rapid responses about the child migrants from Central America. The questions themselves had a tendentious tone: "Why aren't child migrants *immediately* deported?" one of them said, as if baffled or enraged by the fact that the children are not met at the border with catapults that will return them to their home countries. If the questions themselves showed a light bias, the answers were worse. They seemed like something from an openly racist nineteenth-century magazine or a reactionary anti-immigration serial, not the *Times:* "Under a statute adopted with bipartisan support, . . . minors from Central America cannot be deported immediately . . . [but] a United States law *allows* Mexican minors *caught* crossing the border to be sent back quickly." (Note: the majority of children are not "caught"—they turn themselves over to Border Patrol.)

Another question read, "Where are the child migrants coming from?" The answer: "More than three-quarters of the children are from mostly *poor and violent* towns in three countries: El Salvador, Guatemala, and Honduras." The italics are mine, of course, but they underscore the less-than-subtle bias in the portrait of the children: children *caught* while crossing illegally, laws that *permit* their deportation, children who come from the *poor and violent* towns. In short: barbarians who deserve sub-human treatment.

The attitude in the United States toward child migrants is not always blatantly negative, but generally speaking, it is based on a kind of misunderstanding or voluntary ignorance. Debate around the matter has persistently and cynically overlooked the causes of the exodus. When causes are discussed, the general consensus and underlying assumption seem to be that the origins are circumscribed to "sending" countries and their many local problems. No one suggests that the causes are deeply embedded in our shared hemispheric history and are therefore not some distant problem in a foreign country that no one can locate on a map, but in fact a transnational problem that includes the United States— not as a distant observer or passive victim that must now deal with thousands of unwanted children arriving at the southern border, but rather as an active historical participant in the circumstances that generated that problem.

The belief that the migration of all of those children is "their" (the southern barbarians') problem is often so deeply ingrained that "we" (the northern civilization) feel exempt from offering any solution. The devastation of the social fabric in Honduras, El Salvador, Guatemala, and other countries is often thought of as a Central American "gang violence" problem that must be kept on the far side of the border. There is little said, for example, of arms being trafficked from the United States into Mexico or Central America, legally or not; little mention of the fact that the consumption of drugs in the United States is what fundamentally fuels drug trafficking in the continent.

But the drug circuit and its many wars—those openly declared and those that are silenced—are being fought in the streets of San Salvador, San Pedro Sula, Iguala, Tampico, Los Angeles, and Hempstead. They are not a problem circumscribed to a small geographic area. The roots and reach of the current situation branch out across hemispheres and form a complex global network whose size and real reach we can't even imagine. It's urgent that we begin talking about the drug war as a hemispheric war, at least—one that begins in the Great Lakes of the northern United States and ends in the mountains of Celaque in southern Honduras.

It would surely be a step forward for our governments to officially acknowledge the hemispheric dimensions of the problem, acknowledge the connection between such phenomena as the drug wars, gangs in Central America and the United States, the trafficking of arms from the United States, the consumption of drugs, and the massive migration of children from the Northern Triangle to the United States through Mexico. No one, or almost no one, from producers to consumers, is willing to accept their role in the great theater of devastation of these children's lives. To refer to the situation as a hemispheric war would be a step forward because it would oblige us to rethink the very language surrounding the problem and, in doing so, imagine potential directions for combined policies. But of course, a "war refugee" is bad news and an uncomfortable truth for governments, because it obliges them to deal with the problem instead of simply "removing the illegal *aliens.*"

When I ask Manu one day what he thinks of Hempstead, he says it is almost as ugly as Tegucigalpa but at least it was home to Method Man, from the Wu-Tang Clan, and you could get good CDs there. In a later web search, to corroborate the random fact about Method Man, I find that Hempstead is also where Walt Whitman lived for a while, and where the most obese man in the world was born. In the weeks that follow, I buy some books and start reading about the town: it is a broken community that has served as a stage for the Bloods and the Crips for more than forty years. The rapper A+ released a 1999 album called *Hempstead High*. The hit single from the album is called "Enjoy Yourself," and in the final stanza A+ says, "Actin' all wild, unprofessional / Who got beef, I knock teeth out ya smile / But my lyrical lubricant keeps the crowd movin'." I listen to the song on repeat as I ride the train one day on my way to Hempstead—the irony of those words pounding in my head. Certainly, the Barrio 18 of Tegucigalpa would have done much worse than knock out Manu's front teeth, as the Hempstead 18 had done. But I imagine that, in his nights of adolescent rage and desperation, he wonders why, why this story all over again, why he ever came to the United States.

One day in court I tried to explain the phrase "de Guatemala a Guatepeor"—from Guatebad to Guate-worse—to a lawyer. In translation the phrase loses some of its meaning, but it can be glossed this way: almost five thousand kilometers separate Tapachula, the Guatemala-Mexico border town from which La Bestia departs, from New York. Hundreds of thousands of kids have made the journey, tens of thousands have made it to the bor-der, thousands to cities like Hempstead. Why did you come to the United States? we ask. They might ask a similar question: Why did we risk our lives to come to this country? Why did they come when, as if in some circular nightmare, they arrive at new schools, in their new neighborhoods, and find there the very things they were running from?

Thirty-eight: "What do you think will happen if you go back home?" Some months later, in a phone interview with Alina in which I am still trying to put some pieces of the story together, she tells me that she saved up for years to bring her two daughters and Manu to New York. But she decided to stop saving and go into debt to bring Manu as soon as she realized it was no longer a joke.

No longer children's games, she says. They killed his friend in front of him, you know, and I knew he'd be next.

Thirty-nine: "Are you scared to return?" In this same conversation, Alina also tells me that she brought the girls over after some pandilleros from the gang that killed Manu's friend started waiting outside her eldest daughter's school every day, following her slowly back home on motorbikes as she walked along the side of the road, trying not to look back.

Up until then, the idea of letting the children travel alone with a coyote had been unimaginable—crossing borders, mounting La Bestia. Suddenly the idea of allowing them to stay in Tegucigalpa became even more unimaginable.

Forty: "Who would take care of you if you were to return to your home country?" If the answer is no one, the only option you have is to leave and never go back.

Alina contacted the same coyote that brought Manu to the United States and asked him to bring her daughters over. The older of the two girls is nineteen, not a child anymore, Alina explained, so she was separated from her younger sister and put directly in jail with other adults. Alina had to pay $7,500 to get her out of the detention facility as quickly as possible. I don't ask where she's getting all the money. I suppose that her and her husband's entire life savings have all gone into bringing their three teenagers over.

The children who cross Mexico and arrive at the U.S. border are not "immigrants," not "illegals," not merely "undocumented minors." Those children are refugees of a war, and, as such, they should all have the right to asylum. But not all of them have it.

Tell me how it ends, Mamma, my daughter asks me.

I don't know.

Tell me what happens next.

Sometimes I make up an ending, a happy one. But most of the time I just say:

I don't know how it ends yet.

IV

COMMUNITY

In my first semester teaching at Hofstra University, I was assigned a class called, somewhat blandly, Advanced Conversation. The only thing I'd been told about the course was that I needed to speak Spanish with the students. The rest was up to me. Since I wasn't sure what would get students to talk, I started talking to them, on day one, about the undocumented minors immigration crisis—the only current topic that I knew enough about, and that seemed inexhaustible and urgent enough to devote at least a few class meetings to.

During our first encounters the ten students in the class looked at me silently and with a sort of congealed bewilderment, which I usually prefer to attribute to their excess of hormones and lack of sleep rather than to their apathy or my want of better teaching skills. And I think I may have been right this time not to judge them or myself too harshly, too quickly. Midway into the semester, they started to speak up. They began asking difficult questions and started articulating sophisticated opinions. We decided to refer to the class as a "migration think tank" rather than "Spanish conversation." As the weeks passed, one student, who at the beginning of the semester had argued that the United States had too many "internal" problems to deal with the burden of receiving more immigrants, became the most extreme supporter of the idea that the immigration of children into the United States should be conceived of not as a foreign affairs problem, but as a local concern.

Conscious of my own limitations in the subject matter, I brought in experts to talk to us: immigration lawyers, social workers, activists, and political scientists. The semester rolled on, and it seemed to me that for once, a class I was giving was not just following a syllabus but also growing quite naturally out of our group's shared concerns and questions.

United States law guarantees free public education for all children, no matter their nationality or immigration status. Every child living in U.S. territory has this right. But not all children know this, nor do their parents necessarily know it. With the large influx of new migrant children, many schools in the country are overwhelmed, and negligent administrators simply push parents back when they call to ask about enrollment. Many school districts have reacted by creating more obstacles for newcomers. One of those districts is New York's Nassau County, which has the fifth-largest population of migrant children in the country. It is also the district where I work.

Public schools in Nassau County have denied entrance to many children based on their lack of appropriate immigration papers—something that is by all means an illegal practice. In the summer of 2015 the New York State Education Department held a compliance review and in the end determined that no public school was allowed to ask students for immigration documents of any type.

But not all schools are complying. For months now, Alina has been trying to find a different school for Manu. The two girls are not as vulnerable to gang coercion, she thinks, provided that they keep to themselves. But she tells me that Manu can no longer go unnoticed. For a while he was admitted to a school in Long Beach, but then they told him his English wasn't good enough and that he needed to take language classes first. Other schools said he didn't meet the eligibility criteria, or that he's missing some document or another, or that there's simply no space:

They all tell me no, no, and no.

I ask her who "they" are. She's silent for a moment and then says:

Whoever answers the phone when I call a school.

So what happens next? I ask her.

One October morning, my students come to class particularly anxious. While I explain a table of statistics on immigration patterns, they shuffle in their seats, whisper to each other, look around the classroom and out the window. I stop class and ask what is wrong with them—expecting to hear nothing back. But someone at last says:

Nothing, Prof.

Nothing?

Nothing. We just want to tell you something, another says.

What is it? I ask, sure that they will boycott, or that they will ask to leave early that day.

Well, you know how you brought in that professor to talk to us?

Professor Gowrinathan?

Yes, that one.

I remember, of course. Nimmi Gowrinathan came to give us a lecture on the fundamentals of political activism. She insisted that the most important thing was to know how to transform emotional capital—the rage, sadness, and frustration produced by certain social circumstances—into political capital.

Yes, of course I remember that talk.

Well we know how to do it now. We don't want to be voluntourists in our own town anymore. We want to do something that matters.

What do you mean? I ask.

Together, they explain the plan they have meticulously discussed ahead of time. They suggest using our remaining class time to create a political student organization. To stop talking about the problem, one of them says, and start doing something about it. I sit down and pay attention.

Their idea is simple and brilliant: if the immigration crisis started at the u.s.-Mexico border, in southern Arizona or Texas, and then moved up all the way to the ny immigration court, and now there are children and teenage migrants living in the most remote towns of Long Island, it's not going to end there. The crisis will deepen and spread, and things will fall apart, unless all those kids find a way to become quickly and fully integrated. These kids have been through the worst. They arrive to find an unfamiliar country and a new language, but also a group of strangers that they must now call their family. They have to deal with family reunifications, interrupted education, acculturation, and trauma.

Because Long Island, and Nassau County in particular, is so terribly deficient when it comes to public education and services, the private universities in the area have to offer some kind of sustained relief, my students say. We have the space here, the resources, the classrooms, the football fields, and the radio station. The solutions have to be simple and concrete, they say. No "let's empower the migrants" kind of empty jargon. There have to be intensive English classes, college prep sessions, team sports, a radio program, and a civil rights and duties discussion group. They want to partner with organizations such as The Door, in Manhattan, and s.t.r.o.n.g., a nonprofit that focuses on teenagers in Long Island who are particularly vulnerable to falling into gangs.

It only takes a group of ten motivated students to begin making a small difference. Between the ten of them, before my astonished—even disbelieving—eyes, they draft a constitution, appoint duties, and get the university's approval. Their organization is called TIIA—which plays on the Spanish "tía," or "aunt," and stands for Teenage Immigrant Integration Association.

The United States is a country full of holes, and Hempstead in particular is a giant shithole, as Manu says. But it's also a place full of individuals who, out of a sense of duty toward other people, perhaps, are willing to fill those holes in one by one. There are lawyers and activists who work tirelessly to help communities that aren't their own; there are students who, though not at all privileged, are willing to dedicate their time to those even less privileged than themselves.

There are things that can only be understood retrospectively, when many years have passed and the story has ended. In the meantime, while the story continues, the only thing to do is tell it over and over again as it develops, bifurcates, knots around itself. And it must be told, because before anything can be understood, it has to be narrated many times, in many different words and from many different angles, by many different minds.

I started writing this essay in late November of 2015. At the time, my niece was preparing to major in law, interning with The Door, and working at City College for the Politics of Sexual Violence Research Initiative, with one of the most lucid activists in the area. My green card had still not arrived, and my provisional work permit had expired the month before. I was not illegal, but it was illegal for me to work in the United States. I had to resign temporarily from my teaching job just before the final exam period. I would have taken a spontaneous vacation, but leaving fifty college students without a teacher after spending an entire semester with them weighed on me. I investigated further, asking several lawyers if I could continue working without pay. The answer, without a shade of ambiguity, was no: one is not allowed to "volunteer" at a job where one was previously paid while his or her papers are being processed. United States immigration laws are stringent; it would have been an act of total irresponsibility to have tried to find a loophole, especially since it would have put my family's well-being at risk.

Why did you come to the United States? I wondered if I was "allowed" to write—writing is my work, after all. But of course I did write, and will write, because it's what I can do. And I knew that if I did not write this particular story, it would not have made sense to return to writing anything else.

Why did you come to the United States? Perhaps no one knows the real answer. I know that migrants, when they are still on their way here, learn the Immigrant's Prayer. A friend who had been aboard La Bestia for a few days, working on a documentary, read it to me once. I didn't learn the entire thing, but I remember these lines: "Partir es morir un poco / Llegar nunca es llegar"—"To leave is to die a little / To arrive is never to arrive."

I've had to ask so many children: Why did you come? Sometimes I ask myself the same question. I don't have an answer yet. Before coming to the United States, I knew what others know: that the cruelty of its borders was only a thin crust, and that on the other side a possible life was waiting. I understood, some time after, that once you stay here long enough, you begin to remember the place where you originally came from the way a backyard might look from a high window in the deep of winter: a skeleton of the world, a tract of abandonment, objects dead and obsolete.

And once you're here, you're ready to give everything, or almost everything, to stay and play a part in the great theater of belonging. In the United States, to stay is an end in itself and not a means: to stay is the founding myth of this society. To stay in the United States, you will unlearn the universal metric system so you can buy a pound and a half of cooked ham, accept that thirty-two degrees, and not zero, is where the line falls that divides cold and freezing. You might even begin to celebrate the pilgrims who removed the alien Indians, and the veterans who maybe killed other aliens, and the day of a president who will eventually declare a war on all the other so-called aliens. No matter the cost. No matter the cost of the rent, and milk, and cigarettes. The humiliations, the daily battles. You will give every-thing. You will convince yourself that it is only a matter of time before you can be yourself again, in America, despite the added layers of its otherness already so well adhered to your skin. But perhaps you will never want to be your former self again. There are too many things that ground you to this new life.

Why did you come here? I asked one little girl once.

Because I wanted to arrive.

CODA

(Eight Brief Postscripta)

1) Now, it is the year 2017, and I finally have a green
card, and the world is so upside fucking down that
Trump somehow became president of the United
States, and President Enrique Peña Nieto, in Mexico,
restitched the entire Mexican landscape—previously
tattered—to turn it into a warm welcome doormat
for Trumpland.

2) We should have predicted it, but we did not. I should
have foreseen some of it: I am a novelist, which means
my mind is trained to read the world as part of a
narrative plot, where some events foreshadow others.
One early morning, for example, a few months before
the election, I was standing in front of the bathroom
mirror in my Harlem apartment next to my six-
year-old daughter. We were playing with face paint:
yellow stripes on my forehead, green dots on hers, a
blue spot on my nose. At one point, she dug her index
finger into the miniature bucket of white paint, and
as she spread it across her cheeks she said, "Look,

Mamma, now I'm getting ready for when Trump is president. So they won't know we're Mexicans."

3) Many of us are falling apart, and so, it seems, is everything good. Except a few things. There's the TIIA, for example, which, though still small, has become a fully active group. Its first public action took place on September 26, 2016, the same day as the first presidential debate, which, as it happened, was hosted on our campus at Hofstra University. The TIIA students prepared inspired speeches for the protests that would take place on campus the day of the debate. Looking for ways to support them, I went online and ordered them T-shirts that said "Refugees Welcome Here." Last minute, I ordered one for myself, too, though I never wear T-shirts. The TIIA members that day were a riot. A beautiful, messy bunch. Throughout the day, they sent me SMS messages with pictures and videos of their actions on campus. The best picture was one of a student who made a poster saying "Refugees Welcome Here" and stood behind a life-size cardboard replica of a thumbs-up Donald Trump.

4) A few weeks later, the TIIA decided to organize a soccer match and booked one of the better fields on campus for the game. In a rush, we all tried to recruit as many teenagers, recently arrived in Hempstead, as possible.

Only five people arrived: a girl from Honduras and her mother, a Salvadoran boy who was dropped off by his uncle, a boy from Honduras who arrived on public transport from Hempstead. And, to my absolute joy, Manu—whom I'd been trying to contact for some time with little luck and had managed to reach. As we all walked toward the fields together, I noticed hundreds of migrating birds flocking in the autumn sky above us. The strange yet beautiful irony of it. Once we reached the field, Manu was made captain of one team (and was visibly proud of it). A TIIA student was made captain of the other. The final score was 7–10.

When that TIIA soccer match was over, one student offered to drive Manu home and then take me to the station to catch my train back to Manhattan. When we dropped Manu off in front of his house in Hempstead, my student told me something I won't forget: You know, I never thought the kids we've been reading and talking about in abstract all this time would actually be riding in the back seat of my car one day. I'm proud of being part of this.

5) The day Trump won the election, when I finally gathered enough will-power to get out of bed, I put on that "Refugees Welcome Here" T-shirt, made myself a watery coffee, and left my house—long strides down the street, Kendrick Lamar's song "Alright" playing

on repeat on my headphones—feeling like I was ready for anything. I rode the A down to Penn Station to catch my train to Long Island. When I walked into the train car, the first thing I saw was a twenty-something-year-old man wearing a red Make America et cetera cap. I felt a visceral urge to insult him or throw something at him, but I did not. For the better or worse, my body is incapable of reacting aggressively. Instead, I walked over to him, shyly asked him to remove the headphones he was wearing, and then mumbled and stuttered a way-too-emotional sentence about empathy and social responsibility. In response, he laughed loudly in my face. So I took a seat and opened a book, forcing myself not to cry or look scared.

6) When I arrived in the university and walked into a classroom later that day, I noticed my TIIA students there were wearing the same T-shirt I was: "Refugees Welcome Here." And it was hard, at first, not to cry. Difficult not to expose my absolute fragility in front of the group. But a few minutes later, they were all raising their hands, and having crazy ideas, and making wild, revolutionary plans to counter the uncertainty that lay ahead of us. I sat on top of my professor's desk, cross-legged, and listened, and smiled, and maybe even laughed with them.

7) I know it'll take much more than the meteoric enthusiasm of a bunch of college kids to resist the dark
years ahead. But if I have been able to retain some
sanity, it's thanks to a handful of TIIAs organizing
soccer matches and English classes. I look forward
to the TIIAs and their generation. If we all manage
to pull through in these next years, it'll be thanks
to young people who are willing to give their minds
and hearts and bodies to make changes.

There is a young man in the TIIA who immi-
grated from Ghana to Spain when he was little, and
later became a soccer player, and was then brought
over to the U.S. because of his skills, and now leads
the TIIA soccer games—just because, just because he
thinks that's what's right. There's a young woman
who works many shifts to pay her tuition and has
to explain to her boss that yes, she's brown, and
yes, she supports immigrant children, but that she's
also a decent citizen, and even patriotic (if patriotic means loving and defending an inclusive, egal-
itarian country). There's another young man who
brings a skateboard to class and is half Colombian,
half Turkish, and yet fully American at the same
time, and he is developing a complex plan to teach
civil rights and skateboarding to refugee teenagers.
People ask him if he's Catholic or Muslim or what,
and he says he doesn't know but that maybe he'll

be a writer or a photographer one day. And there's a young man who gently combs his right eyebrow with his thumb and says, No Prof, nah-ah, we won't take it, we won't comply. And another young woman who says, Prof, we gotta turn all our emotional shit into political capital, yo!

8) Manu has SIJ status now. He has found a church where he feels welcome, and he has mentors at S.T.R.O.N.G. who have helped him pull through. He's also learning English with the TIIAs, and comes to play soccer on campus sometimes. He told me he wanted his real name to be disclosed in this book, so he could send it to family and friends back in Honduras. But, because he has yet to apply for a green card, and times are dire and volatile, immigration lawyers we consulted thought it best to maintain his anonymity. When I told him this, he said, Okay, fine, no pasa nada. In the meantime, he said, he'll be practicing the art of flight in his front yard in Hempstead:

ACKNOWLEDGMENTS

The stories told in this essay are true. All names of the children I have interviewed in court, as well as specific facts about their biographical information and that of their sponsors, have been changed in order to protect them. The dates of specific events and the order in which they may have occurred have also been modified for the same reason.

I wish to thank John Freeman, who encouraged me to write this essay and published a shorter, earlier version of it in the journal *Freeman's*. I want to thank the following organizations and think tanks: The Door, Safe Passage, S.T.R.O.N.G., the Migration Policy Institute, the Politics of Sexual Violence Initiative, the American Immigration Lawyers Association, and the Teenage Immigrant Integration Association. For her careful legal review, I thank Careen Shannon, a partner at Fragomen, Del Rey, Bernsen & Loewy, LLP (the nation's leading immigration law firm) and a member of the board of directors of Safe Passage Project. For their insights, support, and enthusiasm I want to give special thanks to Rebecca Sosa, Michael Vargas, Angela Hernández, Nimmi Gowrinathan, and Ana Puente, and to the following TIIAs at Hofstra University: Meshack Eshun Addy, Leah Bursky, Lourdes Carballo, Alexi Cohan, Benjamin Cope, Cem Gokhan, Debbie Gómez, Trey Jackson, Pauleen Samantha Jean-Louis, Brandon Jurewicz, Danielle Lewis, Amanda Moncada, Awilda Pena Luna, Jessica Simonelli, Claudia Steel, and Kaleigh Warner.

SOURCES

Beyond the interviews with children and their family members, for my research I used policy reports, fact sheets, documentaries, and newspaper articles and had many e-mail exchanges. These are mentioned below in the order in which they appear and in relation to the sentence(s) in the text that they support.

Page 12.   *Nothing is clear in the initial coverage of the situation—which soon becomes known, more widely, as the 2014 Central American immigration crisis, though others will advocate for the more accurate term "refugee crisis."* Source: Sonia Nazario, "The Children of the Drug Wars: A Refugee Crisis, Not an Immigration Crisis," *New York Times,* July 11, 2014.

Page 14.   *"Protesters, some exercising their open-carry rights, assemble outside of the Wolverine Center in Vassar [Michigan] that would house illegal juveniles to show their dismay for the situation."* . . . *"Thelma and Don Christie (C) of Tucson demonstrate against the arrival of undocumented immigrants in Oracle, Arizona. July 15, 2014."* Sources: Paul Ingram, "Arizona Town Protests Arrival of Undocumented Migrant Kids," Reuters, July 15, 2014. Lindsay Knake, "Protesters Carry AR Rifles, Flags in March against Central American Teens Coming to Vassar," *Michigan Live* (MLive.com), July 15, 2014.

Page 15.   *As she refills his coffee, she tells him that hundreds of migrant kids will be . . . deported that same day back to Honduras, or Mexico, or somewhere.* Source (among several): Associated Press, "Immigrants in New Mexico Deported to Central America," *Washington Post,* July 14, 2014.

Page 16.   *"Looking happy, the deported children exited the airport on an overcast and sweltering afternoon. One by one, they filed into a bus, playing with balloons they had been given."* Source: Gabriel Stargardter, "First U.S. Flight Deports Honduran Kids under Fast-Track Push," Reuters, July 15, 2014.

Page 19.   *. . . the freight trains that cross Mexico, on top of which as many as half a million Central American migrants ride annually.* Source: Rodrigo Dominguez Villegas, "Central American Migrants and 'La Bestia': The Route, Dangers, and Government Responses," Migration Policy Institute, September 10, 2014.

Page 19.   *Thousands have died or been gravely injured aboard La Bestia, either because of the frequent derailments of the old freight trains or because people fall off during the night.* Source: Padre Alejandro Solalinde et al., *La Bestia* (documentary), Miami: Venevision International, 2011.

Page 22.   *In July 2015, for example, the American Immigration Lawyers Association (AILA) filed a complaint after learning that in a detention center in Dilley, Texas, 250 children were mistakenly given adult-strength hepatitis A vaccinations.* Source: Wendy Feliz and George Tzamaras, "Vaccine Overdose of Detained Children Another Sign that Family Detention Must End," American

Immigration Council and American Immigration Lawyers Association, July 4, 2015.

Page 22.   *By law, the maximum time a person can remain in the ice-box is seventy-two hours, but children are often kept for longer, subject not only to the inhumane conditions and frigid temperatures but also to verbal and physical mistreatment.* Sources: *A Guide to Children Arriving at the Border: Laws, Policies and Responses,* American Immigration Council, June 26, 2015; Cindy Carcamo, "Judge Blasts ICE, Says Immigrant Children, Parents in Detention Centers Should Be Released," *Los Angeles Times,* July 25, 2015.

Page 23.   . . . *we see a trail of flags that volunteer groups tie to trees or fences, indicating that there are tanks filled with water there for people to drink as they cross the desert.* Source: In an e-mail exchange, translator Kevin Gerry Dunn, who has worked for volunteer groups, confirmed: "The water tanks with the flags are left by a group called Humane Borders. I believe that they have permission from the government to leave these tanks in designated spots. The problem is that they're big and unwieldy, so they have to be left near main roads, where migrants are much less likely to walk for fear of getting caught. Other groups (the two I know of in Arizona are No More Deaths and Samaritans, though there may be others) leave gallon jugs along migrant paths, where migrants are much more likely to find them. These gallons are regularly slashed by vigilantes and/or Border Patrol. In one instance Border Patrol was caught on video vandalizing a drop (https://www.youtube.com/watch?v=za_Tmt9rSGI)."

Page 25. *Rapes: eighty percent of the women and girls who cross Mexico to get to the U.S. border are raped on the way. The situation is so common that most of them take contraceptive precautions as they begin the journey north.* Source: Erin Siegal McIntyre and Deborah Bonello, "Is Rape the Price to Pay for Migrant Women Chasing the American Dream?" *Fusion*, September 10, 2014.

Page 26. *Abductions: in 2011, the National Human Rights Commission in Mexico published a special report on immigrant abductions and kidnappings, revealing that the number of abduction victims between April and September 2010—a period of just six months—was 11,333.* Source: Comisión Nacional de Derechos Humanos, *Informe especial sobre secuestro de migrantes en México*, February 22, 2011, p. 26.

Page 26. *. . . some sources estimate that, since 2006, around 120,000 migrants have disappeared in their transit through Mexico.* Source: Shaila Rosagel, "Muerte, trata, violación . . . el drama de migrantes en México es peor que el de Europa: ONGs," sinembargo.mx, September 9, 2015.

Page 26. *On August 24, 2010, the bodies of seventy-two Central and South American migrants were found, piled up in a mass grave, at a ranch in San Fernando, Tamaulipas.* Source (among others): Randal C. Archibold, "Victims of Massacre in Mexico Said to Be Migrants," *New York Times*, August 25, 2010. Among the innumerable sources that reported this fact, it is worth highlighting the online "altar" compiled in 2010 by writer and reporter Alma Guillermoprieto, dedicated to the memory of the seventy-two, at 72migrantes.com. The objective of Guillermoprieto's project was to gather as much information as possible about the assassinated migrants and to bring writers and reporters in Mexico together to issue a collective public protest.

Page 28.   *Some are liminal, like the well-known case of a sixteen-year-old boy on the Mexican side of the border who, in 2012, was shot to death by an American officer on the u.s. side who later claimed the boy and other people had thrown rocks at him.* Source (among others): Nigel Duara, "Family of Mexican Boy Killed by Border Patrol Agent Can Sue, Judge Rules," *Los Angeles Times,* July 10, 2015.

Page 29.   *We know, for instance, that civilian vigilantes and owners of private ranches go out to hunt undocumented migrants, either as a matter of conviction or merely for sport.* Source: The Custom Map of Migrant Mortality found at http://www.humaneborders .info/app/map.asp includes name, location, and cause of death for deceased migrants. The causes of death on private land as recorded by medical examiners often imply extreme violence: "blunt force trauma at the head," "complications of multiple blunt force injuries," "gunshot wounds of the head and torso."

Page 29.   *At the forensic institute of Pima County, Arizona, alone, more than 2,200 human remains have been registered since 2001, the majority of which are still unidentified.* Source: Gayatri Parameswaran and Felix Gaedtke, "Identifying Mexico's Many Dead along the u.s. Border," Al Jazeera, March 17, 2015.

Page 36.   . . . *The Door—a Manhattan-based nonprofit that provides kids and teenagers with services ranging from legal assistance to counseling to English and hip-hop classes . . .* Several organizations give legal support to minor-aged migrants, and they trade off days in court. The Door, unlike most of the others, offers services and support for young migrants that extend beyond the immigration process, from medical and psychological support to English, film, and hip-hop classes and professional entertainment.

Page 38.   *Later, in the summer of 2015, it became known that between April 2014 and August 2015, more than 102,000 unaccompanied children had been detained at the border.* Source: Sarah Pierce, "Unaccompanied Child Migrants in U.S. Communities, Immigration Court, and Schools," Migration Policy Institute, October 2015.

Page 40.   *In New York, for example, as early as August 2014, some organizations got together and decided to form an emergency coalition, called the Immigrant Children Advocates' Relief Effort (ICARE).* "In August 2014, in response to the growing number of unaccompanied minors crossing the U.S.'s southern border, seven nonprofit legal service organizations formed the ICARE Coalition. This coalition provides legal representation to the unaccompanied minors who are in removal proceedings before the New York Immigration Court. The coalition includes the Legal Aid Society, The Door, Catholic Charities, Central American Legal Assistance, Make the Road New York, Safe Passage, and Kids in Need of Defense. Of these seven, three—the Legal Aid Society, Make the Road New York, and The Door—rely on volunteers to ensure that there are sufficient resources at court to assist all children in need. Source: "Volunteer in New York City: ICARE," Unaccompanied

Children Resource Center, https://www.uacresources.org/
regionalefforts/item.6849-Volunteer_in_New_York_City.

Page 48.   *For victims of some crimes, real and horrible crimes,
permission to stay in American territory is probably insufficient recompense. But it's better than nothing.* In Mexico's new immigration
law, approved in 2011 after the slaughter of the seventy-two
migrants in Tamaulipas, there is a similar clause guarantee-
ing the right to a visa when a migrant is a victim of or witness
to a crime. But even now it remains unclear in what way this
clause has been implemented. Source: Immigration Law,
section V, article 52, as published in the *Diario Oficial de la
Federación,* May 25, 2011, and amended April 21, 2016.

Page 49.   *The states with the highest number of children released to
sponsors since the crisis was declared are Texas (over 10,000 children),
California (almost 9,000 children), and New York (over 8,000 children).* Source: Sarah Pierce, "Unaccompanied Child Migrants
in U.S. Communities, Immigration Court, and Schools,"
Migration Policy Institute, October 2015, p. 4.

Page 52.   *The procedure by which Mexican children are deported
in this way is called "voluntary return." And, as unbelievable as it may
seem, voluntary return is the most common verdict. Other than a handful of lucky exceptions, all Mexican children are deported under this
procedure.* According to the U.S. Government Accountability
Office, "Data and a random sample of case files from fiscal
year 2014 found that CBP repatriated about 93 percent of
Mexican UAC under age 14 from fiscal years 2009 through
2014 without documenting the basis for decisions." Source:
Unaccompanied Alien Children: Actions Needed to Ensure Children

Receive Required Care in DHS Custody, GAO-15-521, July 14, 2015.

Page 59.   *And what is the charge? Fundamentally, that the child came to the United States without lawful permission and is therefore "removable." Admitting this charge alone leads to deportation unless the child's attorney can find those potential avenues of relief that form a defense against it.* Source: In an e-mail exchange, immigration lawyer Rebecca Sosa explained, "Although the formal charges are uniform, a child's first hearing before the judge varies depending on factors such as whether the child has an attorney, and whether it is a case on the priority docket, which the government has fast-tracked and imposed short deadlines to move the cases along faster."

The process is exceedingly complicated. In an e-mail, immigration lawyer Careen Shannon outlined it briefly as follows: "First the child appears at a hearing in immigration court, admits to the government's allegations that he or she is removable from the United States, and then asks for a 'continuance' of the removal proceeding for the purpose of securing 'special findings' in family court (or juvenile or probate court, depending on the state). The child's proposed guardian must then go to family court and seek an order of custody or guardianship over the child, and must also ask the court to issue the special findings, which must state (1) that the court declares the child dependent on the court, or legally commits or places the child under the custody of either a state agency or department or an individual or entity appointed by a juvenile court or other state court; (2) that reunification with one or both of the child's parents is not viable due to abuse, neglect, abandonment, or a similar basis under state law; and (3) that it would not be in the child's best interest to be returned to his or her country of nationality or country of last habitual residence.

"Once the child has secured the order and the special findings, he or she can file a petition with USCIS seeking SIJ status. If USCIS approves the petition, the child still doesn't have legal immigration status of any sort: all the child has is approval to apply for permanent residence on the basis of having fulfilled the legal criteria for special immigrant juvenile status. The removal proceeding is still active, so the child has to go back to immigration court with evidence that he or she has been approved for SIJ status and ask the court to terminate the removal proceeding. *Then,* with evidence of both the SIJ status approval and the termination of the removal proceeding, the child can apply to USCIS for adjustment of status to permanent residence."

Page 67.   . . . *the majority of children who find a lawyer do appear in court and are granted some form of relief. All the others are deported, either in absentia or in person.* Sarah Pierce, "Unaccompanied Child Migrants in U.S. Communities, Immigration Court, and Schools," Migration Policy Institute, October 2015.

Page 68.   *Because immigration court is a civil court, these child "aliens" are not entitled to the free legal counsel that American law guarantees to persons accused of crimes.* Source: In an e-mail, immigration lawyer Rebecca Sosa explains, "There is no right to legal representation in the immigration context because it is a civil proceeding, and the rights to counsel protections present in the criminal context do not apply. All immigrants seeking immigration benefits or defending their cases have a right to obtain counsel at no expense to the U.S. government,

117

meaning they have to find and pay for their own attorney or find an attorney who will work for free. Also, some undocumented immigrants are eligible for some limited health care benefits, but only until they reach age 19."

Page 75.   *Miguel Hernández has a poem called "Elegy" about the death of a childhood friend.* Source: Miguel Hernández, *The Selected Poems of Miguel Hernández,* edited and translated by Ted Genoways (Chicago: University of Chicago Press, 2001).

Page 77.   *Shortly after the unaccompanied child migrant crisis was declared in the United States, and after a meeting between President Barack Obama and President Enrique Peña Nieto, the Mexican government introduced its new anti-immigration plan, the Programa Frontera Sur.* Sources: "Assessing the Alarming Impact of Mexico's Southern Border Program," Washington Office on Latin America, May 28, 2015; "Así Planea México domar a la bestia," *La Tribuna,* September 6, 2016; Joseph Sorrentino, "How the U.S. 'Solved' the Central American Migrant Crisis," *In These Times,* May 12, 2015; "Programa Frontera Sur: Una Cacería de Migrantes," *Animal Político*/CIDE.

Page 79.   *. . . the State Department has paid the Mexican government tens of millions of dollars to filter the migration of Central Americans.* Source: Sonia Nazario, "Outsourcing a Refugee Crisis: U.S. Paid Mexico Millions to Target Central Americans Fleeing Violence," *Democracy Now,* October 13, 2015.

Page 80.   *. . . since 2014 [Peña Nieto] has deported more Central Americans each year than the United States, more than 150,000 in 2015.* Sources: "Mexico Now Detains More Central

American Migrants than the U.S.," Washington Office on Latin America, June 11, 2015; Natalia Gómez Quintero, "México deporta 150 mil migrantes en 2015," *El Universal,* February 12, 2016.

Page 83.　*A brief, particularly disconcerting article in the* New York Times *in October 2014 postulated a series of questions and rapid responses about the child migrants from Central America.* Source: Haeyoun Park, "Children at the Border," *New York Times,* October 21, 2014.

Page 92.　*Many school districts have reacted by creating more obstacles for newcomers. One of those districts is New York's Nassau County, which has the fifth-largest population of migrant children in the country.* Source: Sarah Pierce, "Unaccompanied Child Migrants in U.S. Communities, Immigration Court, and Schools," Migration Policy Institute, October 2015.

Page 93.　*In the summer of 2015 the New York State Education Department held a compliance review and in the end determined that no public school was allowed to ask students for immigration documents of any type.* Sources: Benjamin Mueller, "Immigrants' School Cases Spur Enrollment Review in New York," *New York Times,* October 22, 2014, and "Requirements Keep Young Immigrants Out of Long Island Classrooms," *New York Times,* October 21, 2014.

Coffee House Press began as a small letterpress operation in 1972 and has grown into an internationally renowned nonprofit publisher of literary fiction, essay, poetry, and other work that doesn't fit neatly into genre categories.

Coffee House is both a publisher and an arts organization. Through our *Books in Action* program and publications, we've become interdisciplinary collaborators and incubators for new work and audience experiences. Our vision for the future is one where a publisher is a catalyst and connector.

LITERATURE
is not the same thing as
PUBLISHING

This project was made possible
through generous support from

THE FRINGE FOUNDATION

Funder Acknowledgments

Coffee House Press is an internationally renowned independent book publisher and arts nonprofit based in Minneapolis, MN; through its literary publications and *Books in Action* program, Coffee House acts as a catalyst and connector—between authors and readers, ideas and resources, creativity and community, inspiration and action.

Coffee House Press books are made possible through the generous support of grants and donations from corporations, foundations, and the many individuals who believe in the transformational power of literature. Coffee House also receives major operating support from the Amazon Literary Partnership, the Jerome Foundation, The McKnight Foundation, and Target Foundation.

Coffee House Press receives additional support from the Elmer L. & Eleanor J. Andersen Foundation; the David & Mary Anderson Family Foundation; the Buuck Family Foundation; the Dorsey & Whitney Foundation; Dorsey & Whitney LLP; the Fringe Foundation; the Knight Foundation; the Rehael Fund of the Minneapolis Foundation; the Matching Grant Program Fund of the Minneapolis Foundation; Mr. Pancks' Fund in memory of Graham Kimpton, the Schwab Charitable Fund; Schwegman, Lundberg & Woessner, P.A.; the US Bank Foundation; VSA Minnesota for the Metropolitan Regional Arts Council; and the Woessner Freeman Family Foundation in honor of Allan Kornblum.

The Publisher's Circle of Coffee House Press

Publisher's Circle members make significant contributions to Coffee House Press's annual giving campaign. Understanding that a strong financial base is necessary for the press to meet the challenges and opportunities that arise each year, this group plays a crucial part in the success of Coffee House's mission.

Recent Publisher's Circle Members Include

Many anonymous donors, Mr. & Mrs. Rand L. Alexander, Suzanne Allen, Patricia A. Beithon, Bill Berkson & Connie Lewallen, E. Thomas Binger & Rebecca Rand Fund of the Minneapolis Foundation, Robert & Gail Buuck, Claire Casey, Louise Copeland, Jane Dalrymple-Hollo, Ruth Stricker Dayton, Jennifer Kwon Dobbs & Stefan Liess, Mary Ebert & Paul Stembler, Chris Fischbach & Katie Dublinski, Kaywin Feldman & Jim Lutz, Sally French, Jocelyn Hale & Glenn Miller, Randy Hartten & Ron Lotz, Jeffrey Hom, Carl & Heidi Horsch, Amy L. Hubbard & Geoffrey J. Kehoe Fund, Kenneth and Susan Kahn, Stephen & Isabel Keating, Kenneth Koch Literary Estate, Allan & Cinda Kornblum, Leslie Larson Maheras, Sarah Lutman & Rob Rudolph, the Carol & Aaron Mack Charitable Fund of the Minneapolis Foundation, George & Olga Mack, Joshua Mack, Gillian McCain, Mary & Malcolm McDermid, Sjur Midness & Briar Andresen, Maureen Millea Smith & Daniel Smith, Peter Nelson & Jennifer Swenson, Alan Polsky, Marc Porter & James Hennessy, Enrique Olivarez, Jr. & Jennifer Komar, Robin Preble, Jeffrey Scherer, Jeffrey Sugerman & Sarah Schultz, Nan G. & Stephen C. Swid, Patricia Tilton, Stu Wilson & Melissa Barker, Warren D. Woessner & Iris C. Freeman, Margaret Wurtele, Joanne Von Blon, and Wayne P. Zink.

For more information about the Publisher's Circle and other ways to support Coffee House Press books, authors, and activities, please visit www.coffeehousepress.org/support or contact us at info@coffeehousepress.org.